THE PLANT-BASED
COOKBOOK

Vegan Recipes to Save Money and Lose Weight

HARPER CLARK

Table of Contents

Introduction

A plant-based diet consists primarily of plant-based foods such as fruits andvegetables, as well as nuts, whole grains, legumes and seeds. It is not a vegetarian or vegan diet because it is possible to eat poultry, beef,eggs, fish, and dairy products, but plant-based foods provide the majority ofyour nutrient intake. On a plant-based diet, there is no set ratio of plant to animal foods, but eating at least 70% of vegetables is a good place to start. The focus should be on plants.

Is it healthy to eat a plant-based diet?

Yes. A plant-based diet is nutrient-dense and high in protein, vitamins, fiber,minerals, and healthy fats. It is considered a very healthy way of eating and can meet all of your nutritional requirements.

Who should follow a plant-based diet?

A plant-based diet can benefit the majority of adults. According to research, plant-based diets can help prevent and treat chronic diseases, as well as reduce reliance on medications. If you have a medical condition, talk to yourdoctor before changing your diet.

How does a plant-based diet provide enough protein?

Avoid associating protein with meat. Tofu, lentils, beans, nuts and nut butters, seeds, and quinoa are all excellent plant-based protein sources. Remember that dairy, eggs, beef, poultry, and fish are all acceptable on aplant-based diet; they just shouldn't be the main course.

How does one begin a plant-based diet?

Starting a plant-based diet may seem overwhelming at first, but take it oneday at a time.

You can do like this:

1. Consume a lot of vegetables. At lunch and dinner, make half of yourplate vegetables. When selecting vegetables, make sure to include a variety of colors. Snack on vegetables with hummus, salsa, or guacamole.

2. Modify your attitude toward meat. Have smaller portions and do notconsider it the main course anymore.

3. Choose healthy fats. Healthy fats can be found in olive oil, olives, nuts and nut butters, seeds, and avocados.

4. At least once a week, cook a vegetarian meal. Prepare these meals with beans, whole grains, and vegetables.

5. Eat whole grains for breakfast. Begin with a grain such as oatmeal, quinoa, buckwheat, or barley. Then top with nuts or seeds and fresh fruit.

6. Opt for greens. Every day, eat a variety of green leafy vegetables like kale, collards, Swiss chard, spinach, and other greens. To retain flavor and nutrients, steam, grill, braise, or stir-fry them.

7. Create a meal around a salad. In a bowl, combine salad greens such as romaine, spinach, Bibb, or red leafy greens. Mix in a variety of other vegetables, fresh herbs, beans, peas, or tofu.

8. For dessert, eat fruit. After a meal, a ripe, juicy peach, a refreshing slice of watermelon, or a crisp apple will satisfy your sweet tooth.

Should there be any plants avoided on a plant-based diet?

A plant-based diet can include any plant.

Breakfast

Almond Plum Oats Overnight

Preparation time: 15-30 Minutes

Cooking time: 0 Minutes

Servings: 1

Ingredients:

- Rolled oats: 60g
- Plums: 3 ripe and chopped
- Almond milk: 300ml
- Chia seeds: 1 tbsp.
- Nutmeg: a pinch
- Vanilla extract: a few drops
- Whole almonds: 1 tbsp. roughly chopped

Directions:

1. Add oats, nutmeg, vanilla extract, almond milk, and chia seeds to abowl and mix well

2. Add in cubed plums and cover and place in the fridge for a night

3. Mix the oats well next morning and add into the serving bowl

4. Serve with your favorite toppings

Nutrition:

Calories: 248 Carbohydrates: 24.7g Proteins: 9.5g Fat: 10.8g

HIGH PROTEIN TOAST

Preparation time: 30 Minutes

Cooking time: 0 Minutes

Servings: 1

Ingredients:

- White bean: 1 drained and rinsed
- Cashew cream: ½ cup
- Miso paste: 1 ½ tbsp.
- Toasted sesame oil: 1 tsp.
- Sesame seeds: 1 tbsp.
- Spring onion: 1 finely sliced
- Lemon: 1 half for the juice and half wedged to serve
- Rye bread: 4 slices toasted

Directions:

1. In a bowl add sesame oil, white beans, miso, cashew cream, and lemonjuice and mash using a potato masher

2. Make a spread

3. Spread it on a toast and top with spring onions and sesame seeds

4. Serve with lemon wedges

Nutrition:

Calories: 332 Carbohydrates: 44.5g Proteins: 14.5g Fat: 9.25g

Hummus Carrot Sandwich

Preparation time: 30 Minutes

Cooking time: 15 Minutes

Servings: 1

Ingredients:

- Chickpeas: 1 cup can drain and rinsed
- Tomato: 1 small sliced
- Cucumber: 1 sliced
- Avocado: 1 sliced
- Cumin: 1 tsp.
- Carrot: 1 cup diced
- Maple syrup: 1 tsp.
- Tahini: 3 tbsp.
- Garlic: 1 clove
- Lemon: 2 tbsp.
- Extra-virgin olive oil: 2 tbsp.
- Salt: as per your need
- Bread slices: 4

Directions:

1. Add carrot to the boiling hot water and boil for 15 minutes

2. Blend boiled carrots, maple syrup, cumin, chickpeas, tahini, olive oil,salt, and garlic together in a blender

3. Add in lemon juice and mix

4. Add to the serving bowl and you can refrigerate for up to 5 days

5. In between two bread slices, spread hummus and place 2-3 slices ofcucumber, avocado, and tomato and serve

Nutrition:

Calories: 490 Carbohydrates: 53.15g Proteins: 14.1g Fat: 27g

Avocado Miso Chickpeas Toast

Preparation time: 30 Minutes

Cooking time: 15 Minutes

Servings: 1

Ingredients:

- Chickpeas: 400g drained and rinsed
- Avocado: 1 medium
- Toasted sesame oil: 1 tsp.
- White miso paste: 1 ½ tbsp.
- Sesame seeds: 1 tbsp.
- Spring onion: 1 finely sliced
- Lemon: 1 half for the juice and half wedged to serve
- Rye bread: 4 slices toasted

Directions:

1. In a bowl add sesame oil, chickpeas, miso, and lemon juice and mashusing a potato masher

2. Roughly crushed avocado in another bowl using a fork

3. Add the avocado to the chickpeas and make a spread

4. Spread it on a toast and top with spring onion and sesame seeds

5. Serve with lemon wedges

Nutrition:

Calories: 456 Carbohydrates: 13.3g Proteins: 14.6g Fat: 26.6g

BANANA MALT BREAD

Preparation time: 30 Minutes

Cooking time: 1 Hour and 20 Minutes

Servings: 1

Ingredients:

- Hot strong black tea: 120ml
- Malt extract: 150g plus extra for brushing
- Bananas: 2 ripe mashed
- Sultanas: 100g & Pitted dates: 120g chopped
- Plain flour: 250g & Soft dark brown sugar: 50g
- Baking powder: 2 tsp.

Directions:

1. Preheat the oven to 140C

2. Line the loaf tin with the baking paper

3. Brew tea and include sultanas and dates to it

4. Take a small pan and heat the malt extract and gradually add sugar toit

5. Stir continuously and let it cook

6. In a bowl, attach flour, salt, and baking powder and now top with sugarextract, fruits, bananas, and tea

7. Mix the batter well and add to the loaf tin

8. Bake the mixture for an hour

9. Brush the bread with extra malt extract and let it cool down beforeremoving from the tin

10. When done, wrap in a foil; it can be consumed for a week

Nutrition:

Calories: 194 Carbohydrates: 43.3g Proteins: 3.4g Fat: 0.3g

Banana Vegan Bread

Preparation time: 30 Minutes

Cooking time: 1 Hour and 15 Minutes

Servings: 1

Ingredients:

- Overripe banana: 3 largest mashed
- All-purpose flour: 200 g
- Unsweetened non-dairy milk: 50 ml
- White vinegar: ½ tsp.
- Ground flaxseed: 10 g
- Ground cinnamon: ¼ tsp.
- Granulated sugar: 140 g
- Vanilla: ¼ tsp.
- Baking powder: ¼ tsp.
- Baking soda: ¼ tsp.
- Salt: ¼ tsp.
- Canola oil: 3 tbsp.
- Chopped walnuts: ½ cup

Directions:

1. Warmth the oven to 350F and line the loaf pan with parchment paper
2. Mash bananas using a fork
3. Take a large bowl, and add in mash bananas, canola oil, oat milk,sugar, vinegar, vanilla, and ground flax seed
4. Also whisk in baking powder, cinnamon, flour, and salt
5. Attach battery to the loaf pan and bake for 50 minutes
6. Remove from pan and let it sit for 10 minutes
7. Slice when completely cooled down

Nutrition:

Calories: 240 Carbohydrates: 40.3g Proteins: 2.8g Fat: 8.2g

Berry Compote Pancakes

Preparation time: 30 Minutes

Cooking time: 13-14 Minutes

Servings: 1

Ingredients:

- Mixed frozen berries: 200g
- Plain flour: 140 g
- Unsweetened almond milk: 140ml
- Icing sugar: 1 tbsp.
- Lemon juice: 1 tbsp.
- Baking powder: 2 tsp.
- Vanilla extract: a dash
- Salt: a pinch
- Caster sugar: 2 tbsp.
- Vegetable oil: ½ tbsp.

Directions:

1. Take a small pan and add berries, lemon juice, and icing sugar
2. Cook the mixture for 10 minutes to give it a saucy texture and setaside
3. Take a bowl and add caster sugar, flour, baking powder, and salt andmix well
4. Add in almond milk and vanilla and combine well to make a batter
5. Take a non-stick pan, and heat 2 teaspoons oil in it and spread it overthe whole surface
6. Attach ¼ cup of the batter to the pan and cook each side for 3-4minutes
7. Serve with compote

Nutrition:

Calories: 463 Carbohydrates: 92g Proteins: 9.4g Fat: 5.2g

Southwest Breakfast Bowl

Preparation time: 30 Minutes

Cooking time: 0 minutes

Servings: 1

Ingredients:

- Mushrooms: 1 cup sliced
- Chopped cilantro: ½ cup
- Chili powder: 1 tsp.
- Red pepper: ½ diced
- Zucchini: 1 cup diced
- Green onion: ½ cup chopped
- Onion: ½ cup
- Vegan sausage: 1 sliced
- Garlic powder: 1 tsp.
- Paprika: 1 tsp.
- Cumin: ½ tsp.
- Salt and pepper: as per your taste
- Avocado: for topping

Directions:

1. Put everything in a bowl and apply gentle heat until vegetables turnbrown

2. Pour some pepper and salt as you like and serve with your favoritetoppings

Nutrition:

Calories: 361 Carbohydrates: 31.6g Proteins: 33.8g Fat: 12.2g

Buckwheat Crepes

Preparation time: 30 Minutes

Cooking time: 25 Minutes

Servings: 1

Ingredients:

- Raw buckwheat flour: 1 cup
- Light coconut milk: 1 and ¾ cups
- Ground cinnamon: ⅛ tsp.
- Flaxseeds: ¾ tbsp.
- Melted coconut oil: 1 tbsp.
- Sea salt: a pinch
- Any sweetener: as per your taste

Directions:

1. Take a bowl and add flaxseed, coconut milk, salt, avocado, and cinnamon

2. Mix them all well and fold in the flour

3. Now take a nonstick pan and pour oil and provide gentle heat

4. Add a big spoon of a mixture

5. Cook till it appears bubbly, and then change side

6. Perform the task until all crepes are prepared

7. For enhancing the taste, add the sweetener of your liking

Nutrition:

Calories: 71 Carbohydrates: 8g Proteins: 1g Fat: 3g

CHICKPEAS SPREAD SOURDOUGH TOAST

Preparation time: 30 Minutes

Cooking time: 0 Minutes

Servings: 1

Ingredients:

- Chickpeas: 1 cup rinsed and drained
- Pumpkin puree: 1 cup
- Vegan yogurt: ½ cup
- Salt: as per your need
- Sourdough: 2 slices toasted

Directions:

1. In a bowl add chickpeas and pumpkin puree and mash using a potatomasher

2. Add in salt and yogurt and mix

3. Spread it on a toast and serve

Nutrition:

Calories: 187 Carbohydrates: 33.7g Proteins: 8.45g Fat: 2.5g

CHICKPEAS WITH HARISSA

Preparation time: 30 Minutes

Cooking time: 0 Minutes

Servings: 1

Ingredients:

- Chickpeas: 1 cup can rinse and drained well
- Onion: 1 small diced
- Cucumber: 1 cup diced
- Tomato: 1 cup diced
- Salt: as per your taste
- Lemon juice: 2 tbsp.
- Harissa: 2 tsp.
- Olive oil: 1 tbsp.
- Flat-leaf parsley
- 2 tbsp. chopped

Directions:

1. Add lemon juice, harissa, and olive oil in a bowl and whisk

2. Take a serving bowl and add onion, cucumber, chickpeas, salt and thesauce you made

3. Add parsley from the top and serve

Nutrition:

Calories: 398 Carbohydrates: 55.6g Proteins: 17.8g Fat: 11.8g

Quinoa Quiche Cups

Preparation time: 5 minutes

Cooking time: 20 minutes

Servings: 6

Ingredients:

- 1 (10-ounce) bag frozen mixed vegetables, thawed
- ¾ cup quinoa flour
- ¾ cup water
- 2 tablespoons freshly squeezed lemon juice
- ¼ cup nutritional yeast
- ¼ teaspoon granulated garlic
- ¼ teaspoon sea salt
- Freshly ground black pepper

Directions:

1. In a medium bowl, mix the vegetables, quinoa flour, water, lemon juice, nutritional yeast, granulated garlic, salt, and pepper to taste untilwell combined.

2. Spoon the mixture into 6 cupcake molds, dividing it evenly.

3. Place the filled molds into the air fryer and bake at 340F for 20 minutes. Let cool slightly before enjoying.

Nutrition:

Calories: 239 Fat: 2g Carbohydrates: 39g Fiber: 8g Proteins: 16g

FRENCH TOAST

Preparation time: 5 minutes

Cooking time: 10 minutes

Servings: 4

Ingredients:

- 1 ripe banana, mashed
- ¼ cup protein powder
- ½ cup plant-based milk
- 2 tablespoons ground flaxseed
- 4 slices whole-grain bread
- Nonstick cooking spray

Directions:

1. In a shallow bowl, mix the banana, protein powder, plant-based milk,and flaxseed until well combined.

2. Set both sides of each slice of bread into the mixture. Lightly spray your pan or air fryer basket with oil and place the slices on it in a singlelayer. Pour any remaining mixture evenly over the bread.

3. Bring the pan in the air fryer and fry at 370F for 10 minutes, or untilgolden brown and crispy. Be sure to flip the toast over halfway through. Enjoy the warmth.

Nutrition:

Calories: 365 Fat: 11g Carbohydrates: 48g Fiber: 9g Proteins: 22g

BLUEBERRY-BANANA MUFFINS

Preparation time: 16 minutes

Cooking time: 16 minutes

Servings: 6

Ingredients:

- 1 ripe banana
- ½ cup unsweetened plant-based milk
- 1 teaspoon apple cider vinegar
- 1 teaspoon vanilla extract
- 2 tablespoons ground flaxseed
- 2 tablespoons coconut sugar
- ¾ cup all-purpose flour
- 1 teaspoon baking powder
- ½ teaspoon baking soda
- ¾ cup blueberries

Directions:

1. In a medium bowl, press the banana with a fork. Add the plant-based milk, apple cider vinegar, vanilla, flaxseed, and coconut sugar and mixuntil well combined. Set aside.

2. In a small bowl set together the flour, baking powder, and baking soda.Add this mixture to the medium bowl and mix until just combined. (Over mixing will make the muffins tough.)

3. Pour the batter into 6 cupcake molds, dividing it evenly. Then dividethe blueberries evenly among the muffins and lightly press them intothe batter so that they are at least partially submerged.

4. Place the molds in the air fryer and bake at 350°F for 16 minutes. Letcool before enjoying.

Nutrition:

Calories: 248 Fat: 3g Carbohydrates: 50g Fiber: 4g Proteins: 6g

Apple Pie Oat Bowls

Preparation time: 12 minutes

Cooking time: 6 minutes

Servings: 2

Ingredients:

- ⅔ cup rolled oats
- 1 apple, cored and diced
- 4 dates, pitted and diced
- ½ teaspoon ground cinnamon
- ¾ cup unsweetened plant-based milk

Directions:

1. In a heatproof cake pan or bowl, combine the oats, apple, dates, andcinnamon. Pour the plant-based milk over the top.

2. Bring the pan in the air fryer and bake at 350F for 6 minutes. Removethe pan and stir until well mixed. Bake for another 6 minutes until theapples are soft.

3. Stir again and let cool slightly before enjoying.

Nutrition:

Calories: 222 Fat: 3g Carbohydrates: 44g Fiber: 7g Proteins: 7g

Hash Browns

Preparation time: 12 minutes

Cooking time: 12 minutes

Servings: 4

Ingredients:

- 3 cups frozen shredded potatoes, thawed
- 2 tablespoons nutritional yeast
- 1 teaspoon No-Salt Spice Blend
- 1 tablespoon Aquafina
- 1 Cut 4 pieces of parchment paper, each about 12 inches long.

Directions:

1. In a medium bowl, mix the potatoes, nutritional yeast, spice blend, and Aquafina until well combined. Divide the mixture into 4 equal portions.

2. Place 1 portion onto the middle of a piece of parchment paper. Fold thesides of the paper together and then the top and bottom to create a rectangle about 3 by 5 inches. With the use of your hand, push down onthe hash brown to flatten and spread it.

3. Unwrap the parchment paper and use a spatula to carefully transfer thehash brown to the air fryer basket or rack. Repeat step 3 with the remaining portions.

4. Fry the hash browns at 400F for 12 minutes, or until they are lightly browned and crispy. Be sure to flip the hash browns halfway throughcooking. Enjoy the warmth.

Nutrition:

Calories: 92 Fat: 0g Carbohydrates: 20g Fiber: 3g Proteins: 3g

APPLE-CINNAMON BREAKFAST COOKIES

Preparation time: 5 Minutes

Cooking time: 9 Minutes

Servings: 15

Ingredients:

- 1 medium apple
- 1 cup oat flour
- 2 tablespoons pure maple syrup
- ¼ cup natural peanut butter
- ⅓ cup raisins
- ½ teaspoon ground cinnamon

Directions:

1. Using a grater or a julienne mandolin, carefully grate each side of the apple down to the core. Bring the grated apple in a medium bowl alongwith the oat flour, maple syrup, peanut butter, raisins and cinnamon. Mix until well combined.

2. Scoop out 2-tablespoon balls of dough onto parchment paper. Wet yourhand to avoid sticking and flatten each cookie.

3. Bring the cookies from the parchment paper to the air fryer basket orrack and bake at 350F for 9 minutes, or until the edges of the cookiesstart to brown. Enjoy the warmth.

Nutrition:

Calories: 384 Fat: 14g Carbohydrates: 58g fiber: 6g Proteins: 11g

Cinnamon Rolls

Preparation time: 10 minutes

Cooking time: 8 minutes

Servings: 8

Ingredients:

- ½ (16-ounce) frozen pizza dough, thawed
- ⅓ cup Date Paste
- ¼ cup natural peanut butter
- ½ teaspoon ground cinnamon
- Nonstick cooking spray

Directions:

1. With a sheet of parchment paper, set out the pizza dough to about a 6-by-9-inch rectangle.

2. Spread the date paste and peanut butter evenly over the dough, covering it all the way to the edges. Then sprinkle the cinnamon evenlyon top.

3. Roll the dough into a log. Set the log into 8 equal pieces, being carefulnot to compress the dough too much.

4. Place the pieces, spiral-side up, in your air fryer basket or on a flat tray.Let the dough rest and rise.

5. Lightly spray the rolls with cooking spray. Bake at 360F for 8 minutes,or until lightly browned. Serve warm.

Nutrition:

Calories: 270 Fat: 10g Carbohydrates: 39g Fiber: 3g Proteins: 9g

Tofu Scramble Brunch Bowls

Preparation time: 10 minutes

Cooking time: 15 minutes

Servings: 2

Ingredients:

- 1 medium russet potato, cut into fries or 1-inch cubes
- 1 bell pepper, seedless and cut into 1-inch strips
- ½ (14-ounce) block medium-firm tofu, drained and cubed
- 1 tablespoon nutritional yeast
- ½ teaspoon granulated garlic
- ½ teaspoon granulated onion
- ¼ teaspoon ground turmeric
- 1 tablespoon apple cider vinegar

Directions:

1. Place the potato and pepper strips in the air fryer basket or on the rackand fry at 400°F for 10 minutes.

2. Meanwhile, in a small pan, place the tofu, nutritional yeast, granulatedgarlic, granulated onion, turmeric and apple cider vinegar and stir gently to combine.

3. Add the pan to the air fryer, on a rack above the potatoes and peppers.Continue to fry at 400F for an additional 5 minutes, or until the potatoes are crispy and the tofu is heated through.

4. Detach the food from the air fryer and stir the tofu in the pan. Divide the potatoes and peppers evenly between 2 bowls. Then spoon half thetofu over each bowl. Serve warm.

Nutrition:

Calories: 267 Fat: 6g Carbohydrates: 42g Fiber: 4g Proteins: 15g

PB and J Power Tarts

Preparation time: 15 minutes

Cooking time: 8 minutes

Servings: 2

Ingredients:

- ¼ cup natural peanut butter
- 1 tablespoon coconut sugar
- 2 tablespoons unsweetened coconut yogurt
- ½ cup oat flour
- 2 tablespoons Blueberry Fruit Spread

Directions:

1. Cut 2 pieces of parchment paper, each 8 inches long. On one of thepieces of parchment paper, measure out and draw a 5-by-12-inch rectangle.

2. In a medium bowl, merge the peanut butter, coconut sugar, and coconutyogurt. Once they are combined, mix in the oat flour to form dough.

3. Place the dough on the blank piece of parchment paper and cover it with the other piece, with the rectangle facing you. Use a rolling pin toevenly set out the dough to fit in the rectangle. Carefully peel off the top piece of parchment paper.

4. Set the dough into 4 equal rectangles, each 3 by 5 inches. Place 1 tablespoon of the fruit spread on 2 of the rectangles and spread it outevenly. Carefully place the remaining 2 rectangles on top of the fruitspread and gently press on the edges with a fork.

5. Place the tarts in the air fryer basket or on the rack and bake at 350F for8 minutes. Enjoy the warmth.

Nutrition:

Calories: 358 Fat: 19g Carbohydrates: 38g Fiber: 4g Proteins: 12g

Avocado Bagels

Preparation time: 25 minutes

Cooking time: 10 minutes

Servings: 2

Ingredients:

- ⅔ cup all-purpose flour & ½ teaspoon active dry yeast
- ⅓ cup unsweetened coconut yogurt
- 8 cherry or grape tomatoes
- 1 ripe avocado & 1 tablespoon freshly squeezed lemon juice
- 2 tablespoons finely chopped red onion
- Freshly ground black pepper

Directions:

1. In a bowl, merge the flour, yeast, and coconut yogurt. Knead intosmooth dough. Divide the dough into 2 equal balls. Roll each ball into a 9-inch-longrope. Then form a ring with each rope and press the ends together toconnect them, creating 2 bagels.

2. Fill a medium bowl with hot (but not boiling) water. Soak the bagels inthe water for 1 minute. Then shake off the excess water and move themto the air fryer basket or rack to rise for 15 minutes. Bake at 400F for 5 minutes. Then flip the bagels over and add thetomatoes to the air fryer basket. Bake for an additional 5 minutes. 5 Meanwhile, cut the avocado in half and carefully remove the pit. Scoop the avocado out into a small bowl and mash it with a fork. Mixin the lemon juice and red onion.

3. Let the bagels cool slightly before cutting them in half. Divide the avocado mixture among the 4 bagel halves. Top each bagel half with 2 baked tomatoes and season with pepper.

Nutrition:

Calories: 375 Fat: 16g Carbohydrates: 52g Fiber: 9g Proteins: 9g

SAMOSA ROLLS

Preparation time: 15 minutes

Cooking time: 15 minutes

Servings: 8

Ingredients:

- ⅔ cup frozen peas, thawed
- 4 scallions, both white and green parts
- 2 cups grated sweet potato
- 2 tablespoons freshly squeezed lemon juice
- 1 teaspoon ground ginger
- 1 teaspoon curry powder
- ¼ cup chickpea flour
- 1 tablespoon tahini & ⅓ cup water
- 8 (6-inch) rice paper wrappers

Directions:

1. In a medium bowl, combine the peas, scallions, sweet potato, lemonjuice, ginger, curry powder, and chickpea flour. Set aside. In a small bowl, merge the tahini and water until well combined. Pourthe mixture onto a plate.

2. Dip both sides of a rice paper wrapper into the tahini mixture. Whenthe wrapper starts to soften up, transfer it to another plate.

3. Spoon one-eighth of the filling (about ⅓ cups) onto the wrapper andwrap it up tightly, burrito style. Place the roll, seam-side down, in theair fryer basket or on the rack, and redo this process.

4. Bake at 350F for 15 minutes until the wrappers are lightly browned and crispy. Flip the rolls over halfway through cooking. Serve warm.

Nutrition:

Calories: 222 Fat: 6g Carbohydrates: 43g Fiber: 5g Proteins: 3g

TOFU-SPINACH SCRAMBLE

Preparation time: 15 minutes

Cooking time: 15-16 minutes

Servings: 5

Ingredients:

- 1(14-ounce) package water-packed extra-firm tofu
- 1 tsp. extra-virgin olive oil & 1 small yellow onion, diced
- 3 teaspoons minced garlic (about 3 cloves)
- 3 large celery stalks, chopped
- 2 large carrots, peeled (optional) and chopped
- 1 teaspoon chili powder & ½ teaspoon ground cumin
- ½ teaspoon ground turmeric & ½ teaspoon salt (optional)
- ¼ teaspoon freshly ground black pepper
- 5 cups loosely packed spinach

Directions:

1. Drain the tofu by placing it, wrapped in a paper towel on a plate in thesink. Place a cutting board over the tofu, then set a heavy pot, can, or cookbook on the cutting board. Remove after 10 minutes. (Alternatively, use a tofu press).

2. In a medium bowl, crumble the tofu with your hands or a potato masher. Heat the olive oil. Add the onion, garlic, celery, and carrots, and sautéfor 5 minutes until the onion is softened.

3. Add the crumbled tofu, chili powder, cumin, turmeric, salt (if using),and pepper, and continue cooking for 7 to 8 more minutes, stirring frequently, until the tofu begins to brown.

4. Add the spinach and mix well. Cover and reduce the heat to medium.Steam the spinach for 3 minutes. Divide evenly among 5 single-serving containers. Let cool beforesealing the lids.

Nutrition:

Calories: 122 Fat: 15g Proteins: 14g Carbohydrates: 54g Fiber: 8g

SAVORY PANCAKES

Preparation time: 10 minutes

Cooking time: 15 minutes

Servings: 4

Ingredients:

- 1 cup whole-wheat flour
- 1 teaspoon garlic salt
- 1 teaspoon onion powder
- ½ teaspoon baking soda
- ¼ teaspoon salt
- 1 cup lightly pressed, crumbled soft or firm tofu
- ½ cup unsweetened plant-based milk
- ¼ cup lemon juice
- 2 tablespoons extra-virgin olive oil
- ½ cup finely chopped mushrooms
- ½ cup finely chopped onion
- 2 cups tightly packed greens (arugula, spinach, or baby kale workgreat)

Directions:

1. Attach the flour, garlic salt, onion powder, baking soda, and salt. Mix well. In a blender, combine the tofu, plant-based milk, lemon juice, andolive oil. Purée at high speed for 30 seconds.

2. Spill the contents of the blender into the bowl of the dry ingredients and whisk until combined well. Fold in the mushrooms, onion, and greens.

Nutrition:

Calories: 132 Fat: 10g Proteins: 12g Carbohydrates: 44g Fiber: 9g

ENGLISH MUFFINS WITH TOFU

Preparation time: 10 minutes

Cooking time: 15 minutes

Servings: 4

Ingredients:

- 2 tablespoons olive oil
- 16 ounces extra-firm tofu
- 1 tablespoon nutritional yeast
- ¼ teaspoon turmeric powder
- 2 handfuls fresh kale, chopped
- Kosher salt and ground black pepper, to flavor
- 4 English muffins, cut in half
- 4 tablespoons ketchup
- 4 slices vegan cheese

Directions:

1. Warmth the olive oil in a frying skillet over medium heat. When it's hot, add the tofu and sauté for 8 minutes, stirring occasionally to promote even cooking.

2. Add in the nutritional yeast, turmeric and kale and continue sautéing an additional 2 minutes or until the kale wilts. Season with salt and pepperto taste.

3. Meanwhile, toast the English muffins until crisp.

4. To assemble the sandwiches, spread the bottom halves of the English muffins with ketchup; top them with the tofu mixture and vegan cheese; place the bun topper on, close the sandwiches and serve warm.

5. Bon appétit!

Nutrition:

Calories: 150 Fat: 7.3g Fiber: 6.1g Carbohydrates: 18g Proteins: 3.7g

MULTIGRAIN HOT CEREAL WITH APRICOTS

Preparation time: 30 minutes

Cooking time: 17 minutes

Servings: 2

Ingredients:

- ¼ cup long-grain brown rice
- 2 tablespoons rye
- 2 tablespoons millet
- 2 tablespoons wheat berries
- 2 tablespoons barley
- 6 dried apricots, chopped
- 2 cups water

Directions:

1. Clean the grains and soak them in water for 30 minutes until softenedand drain.

2. In a saucepan, add the soaked grains, apricots, and 2 cups of water andstir to combine.

3. Cook for about 17 minutes over low heat, or until the liquid isabsorbed, stirring periodically.

4. Allow to cool before serving.

Nutrition:

Calories: 242 Fat: 1.6g Carbohydrates: 50.5g Proteins: 6.5g Fiber: 6.1g

Cinnamon Pear Oatmeal

Preparation time: 10 minutes

Cooking time: 15 minutes

Servings: 22

Ingredients:

- 3 cups water
- 1 cup steel-cut oats
- 1 tbsp. cinnamon powder
- 1 cup pear, cored and peeled, cubed

Directions:

1. Take a pot and attach the water, oats, cinnamon, and pear and tosswell. Bring it to parboil over medium heat.

2. Let it cook for 15 minutes and set into two bowls.

3. Enjoy!

Nutrition:

Calories: 365 Fat: 11g Carbohydrates: 48g Fiber: 9g

Hearty Pineapple Oatmeal

Preparation time: 10 minutes

Cooking time: 4-8 hours

Servings: 4

Ingredients:

- 1 cup steel-cut oats
- 4 cups unsweetened almond milk
- 2 medium apples, sliced
- 1 teaspoon coconut oil
- 1 teaspoon cinnamon
- ¼ teaspoon nutmeg
- 2 tablespoons maple syrup, unsweetened
- A drizzle of lemon juice

Directions:

1. Attach listed ingredients to a cooking pan and mix well. Cook on verylow flame for 8 hours/or on high flame for 4 hours.

2. Gently stir. Attach your desired toppings.

3. Serve and enjoy!

Nutrition:

Calories: 332 Carbohydrates: 44.5g Proteins: 14.5g Fat: 9.25g

Cool Mushroom Munchies

Preparation time: 5 minutes.

Cooking time: 10 minutes.

Servings: 2

Ingredients:

- 4 Portobello mushroom caps
- 3 tablespoons coconut amines
- 2 tbsp. sesame oil
- 1 tbsp. fresh ginger, minced
- 1 small garlic clove, minced

Directions:

1. Set your broiler to low, keeping the rack 6 inches from the heating source. Rinse mushrooms under cold water and transfer them to abaking sheet (top side down).

2. Take a bowl and merge in sesame oil, garlic, coconut aminos, gingerand pour the mixture over the mushrooms tops.

3. Cook for 10 minutes. Serve and enjoy!

Nutrition:

Calories: 248 Fat: 3g Carbohydrates: 50g Fiber: 4g

Lunch

French Onion Soup

Preparation time: 10 minutes.

Cooking time: 50 minutes.

Servings: 4

Ingredients:

- 4 medium onions, yellow or red, thinly sliced
- 3 tablespoons balsamic vinegar
- 3 cups vegetable stock
- 1 tablespoon dried thyme
- 3 dried bay leaves

Directions:

1. In a large nonstick saucepan, sauté the onions, stirring occasionally andadding 1 tablespoon of water at a time to prevent sticking, for about 25minutes or until the onions are translucent and caramelized.

2. Add the vinegar and sauté for 5 more minutes, until the onions darkenin color.

3. Attach the stock, 2 cups of water, the thyme, and bay leaves.

4. Cover and simmer for 20 minutes, until thickened.

5. Remove from the heat and discard the bay leaves.

6. Serve hot.

7. Serving Tip: For an authentic presentation, you can make bread tops for thissoup. Use slices of a whole-grain baguette, top with a dollop of my Cheesy Sauce, and broil on high for 4 minutes.

Nutrition:

Calories: 68 Fat: 1g Proteins: 1g Carbohydrates: 15g Fiber: 2g

LASAGNA SOUP

Preparation time: 10 minutes.

Cooking time: 15 minutes.

Servings: 4

Ingredients:

- 2 cups mini whole-grain lasagna noodles
- 1 (26-ounce) can diced tomatoes
- 2 cups Mushroom Crumble
- 2½ tablespoons Italian seasoning
- 1 tablespoon garlic powder

Directions:

1. Set 5 cups of water to a boil and attach the pasta noodles. Boil for 6minutes.

2. Set the heat to medium and attach the tomatoes, mushroom crumble, Italian seasoning, and garlic powder. Stir to combine.

3. Simmer for 5 minutes, until fragrant.

4. Detach from the heat and serve warm or allow cooling and refrigeratingin an airtight container for up to 3 days.

Nutrition:

Calories: 244 Fat: 2g Proteins: 11g Carbohydrates: 50g Fiber: 10g

BLACK BEAN AND MUSHROOM STEW

Preparation time: 10 minutes.

Cooking time: 20 minutes.

Servings: 5

Ingredients:

- 7 cups sliced mushrooms (about 1 pound)
- 3 cups vegetable stock
- 1 (19-ounce) can black beans (about 2 cups cooked), rinsed and drained
- 3 tablespoons tomato paste
- 3 tablespoons Savory Spice

Directions:

1. In a nonstick saucepan over medium-high heat, sauté the mushrooms for 10 minutes, until soft and brown. Stir often to avoid sticking. Attachthe stock, 1 tablespoon at a time, if needed to prevent sticking.

2. Attach the beans to the pan, along with the tomato paste and savoryspice. Stir to combine.

3. Set to a boil over high heat, set the heat to low, cover, and simmer for 8minutes. Stir occasionally.

4. Serve hot.

Nutrition:

Calories: 181 Fat: 1g Proteins: 14g Carbohydrates: 32g Fiber: 10g

SPICY PEANUT RAMEN

Preparation time: 5 minutes.

Cooking time: 10 minutes.

Servings: 4

Ingredients:

- 4 servings brown rice ramen noodles
- ½ cup Peanut Sauce
- 1 tablespoon Shichimi Togarashi Spice Mix
- 1 cup cooked edamame beans
- ½ cup chopped scallions

Directions:

1. Cook the noodles.

2. Meanwhile, in a nonstick pan, combine the peanut sauce, spice mix,beans, and ½ cup of water. Set the heat to medium and stew for 5 minutes, stirring occasionally, until warmed.

3. Drain the noodles and divide among 4 bowls.

4. Top with the warmed peanut sauce and edamame. Garnish with thescallions.

5. Serve immediately.

Nutrition:

Calories: 333 Fat: 9g Proteins: 13g Carbohydrates: 53g Fiber: 5g

CREAMY MUSHROOM SOUP

Preparation time: 10 minutes.

Cooking time: 20 minutes.

Servings: 4

Ingredients:

- 5 cups sliced mushrooms
- 5 garlic cloves, minced
- 1½ cups vegetable stock
- 1½ cups unsweetened plant-based milk
- 1 tablespoon dried thyme

Directions:

1. Warmth a deep nonstick pan over medium-high heat and sauté the mushrooms and garlic for 10 minutes or until the mushrooms are soft. Attach ¼ cup of water if the pan gets too dry.

2. Mix in the stock, plant-based milk, and thyme.

3. Set the heat to low and stew for 8 minutes, stirring occasionally, untilthe soup thickens.

4. Serve warm.

Nutrition:

Calories: 46 Fat: 1g Proteins: 3g Carbohydrates: 7g Fiber: 1g

POTATO HARVEST STEW

Preparation time: 10 minutes.

Cooking time: 15 minutes.

Servings: 5

Ingredients:

- 3 cups chopped, unpeeled yellow potatoes
- 1 cup sliced carrots
- 1 small yellow onion, diced
- 3 tablespoons tomato paste
- 1½ tablespoons poultry seasoning

Directions:

1. In a large stockpot, bring the potatoes and carrots to boil in 6 cups ofwater. Boil for 8 minutes.

2. Meanwhile, in a nonstick pan, sauté the onion.

3. Reserving 3 cups of the boiling water drains the potatoes and carrots.

4. In the stockpot, combine the reserved cooking water, tomato paste, andpoultry seasoning. Stir to combine. Set to a boil over high heat and thenreduce the heat to low.

5. Add the potatoes, carrots, and onion. Remove from the heat.

6. Serve warm.

Nutrition:

Calories: 114 Fat: 1g Proteins: 3g Carbohydrates: 26g Fiber: 4g

Quick Black Bean Chili

Preparation time: 5 minutes.

Cooking time: 20 minutes.

Servings: 5

Ingredients:

- 1 (15-ounce) can diced tomatoes
- 1 (19-ounce) can black beans, rinsed and washed
- 1½ cups tomato sauce
- 2 cups Mushroom Crumble
- 3 tablespoons Chipotle Spice

Directions:

1. In a pot with a lid, combine the tomatoes, black beans, tomato sauce,mushroom crumble, and chipotle spice. Stir.

2. Set to a boil over high heat and then set the heat to low. Cover and simmer, stirring occasionally, until fragrant, about 20 minutes.

3. Serve warm or allow cooling.

Nutrition:

Calories: 199 Fat: 1g Proteins: 13g Carbohydrates: 37g Fiber: 13g

Sweet Potato and Peanut Stew

Preparation time: 15 minutes.

Cooking time: 30 minutes.

Servings: 4

Ingredients:

- 2 onions, diced
- 2 tablespoons extra-virgin olive oil or coconut oil
- 2 large sweet potatoes, peeled and chopped
- ⅓ cup chunky peanut butter
- 1 teaspoon smoked paprika
- ¼ tsp. red pepper flakes
- 2 cups water or unsalted vegetable broth
- ¼ teaspoon salt
- 2 cups finely chopped fresh spinach or kale
- Freshly ground black pepper

Directions:

1. On your electric pressure cooker, select Sauté. Add the onions and olive oil, and then cook for 4-5 minutes, stirring occasionally, until theonion has softened. Stir in the sweet potatoes, peanut butter, paprika, chili flakes, water and salt. Stir to mix the peanut butter with the watera little, but don't worry too much as it will melt when heated. Cancel Sauté.

2. High pressure for 6 minutes, close and lock the lid and make sure thepressure valve is sealed and set the time to 6 minutes.

3. Releasing the pressure. At the end of the

4. Cooking time, quickly releasethe pressure. Once all pressure has been released, carefully unlock and remove the lid. Incorporate the spinach to wilt. Set and season with more salt and pepper.

Nutrition:

Calories: 350 Proteins: 10g Fat: 18g Carbohydrates: 16g Fiber: 8g

Split Pea Soup

Preparation time: 10 minutes.

Cooking time: 30 minutes.

Servings: 6

Ingredients:

- 3 or 4 carrots, scrubbed or peeled and chopped
- 1 large yellow onion, chopped
- 1 cup dried split green peas
- 3 cups water or unsalted vegetable broth
- 1 tablespoon tamari or soy sauce
- 2 to 3 teaspoons dried thyme or 1 teaspoon ground thyme
- 1 teaspoon onion powder
- ½ teaspoon garlic powder
- Pinch freshly ground black pepper
- ¼ cup chopped sun-dried tomatoes or chopped pitted black olives
- Salt

Directions:

1. In the electric pressure cooker, combine the carrots, onion, split peas,water, tamari, thyme, onion powder, garlic powder and pepper.

2. High pressure for 10 minutes. Secure and lock the lid and make sure the pressure valve is sealed, then select High pressure and set the timeto 10 minutes.

3. Relief of pressure. Once the

4. Cooking time is done, let the pressure naturally release for about 20 minutes. Once all pressure is released, carefully unlock and remove the lid. Let it cool then blend the soup: use an immersion blender directly into the pot.

Nutrition:

Calories: 182 Proteins: 12g Fat: 1g Carbohydrates: 26g Fiber: 12

SOUR SOUP

Preparation time: 5 minutes

Cooking time: 20 minutes

Servings: 4

Ingredients:

- 2 tablespoons dried wood ears
- 3.5ounces bamboo shoots, sliced into thin strips
- 1 medium carrot, peeled, sliced into thin strips
- 5 dried shiitake mushrooms
- 1 tablespoon grated ginger
- 1 teaspoon minced garlic
- 1 teaspoon ground black pepper
- 1 teaspoon salt
- ¼ cup soy sauce
- 1 teaspoon sugar
- ½ cup rice vinegar
- 4 cups vegetable stock
- 1 ½ cup water, boiling
- 7.5ounces tofu, extra-firm, drained
- 1 tablespoon green onion tops, chopped
- ¼ cup water, at room temperature
- 2 tablespoons cornstarch
- 1 teaspoon sesame oil

Directions:

1. Take a small bowl, put some wooden ears in it, then pour the boilingwater until it is covered and let it rest for 30 minutes.

2. In the meantime, take another bowl, put the mushrooms in it, pour 1 ½cups of water and let the mushrooms rest for 30 minutes.

3. After 30 minutes, drain the ears of wood, rinse them well and cut theminto slices, remove and discard the hard pieces.

4. Similarly, drain the mushrooms, reserving their soaking liquid and slicethe mushrooms, removing and discarding their stems.

5. Take a large pot, put it on medium-high heat, add the whole Shopping

6. List: including the reserved mushroom liquid, leave the last five Shopping List: mix well and bring to a boil.

7. Then bring the heat to medium and simmer the soup for 10 minutes until cooked.

8. Meanwhile, put the cornstarch in a bowl, add the room temperature water and mix well until smooth.

9. Cut the tofu into 1-inch pieces, add it to the hot soup along with the cornstarch mixture, and continue to simmer the soup until it reaches the desired thickness.

10. Drizzle with sesame oil, spread soup into bowls, garnish with green onions and serve.

Nutrition:

Calories: 152 Fat: 2g Carbohydrates: 35g Proteins: 4g Fiber: 8g

ROASTED TOMATO SOUP

Preparation time: 10 minutes.

Cooking time: 50 minutes.

Servings: 4

Ingredients:

- 2 pounds ripe tomatoes, cored and halved
- 2 large garlic cloves, crushed
- 3 tablespoons extra-virgin olive oil
- 1 tablespoon balsamic vinegar
- Salt and freshly ground black pepper
- ½ cup chopped red onion
- 2 cups light vegetable broth or store-bought, or water
- ½ cup lightly packed fresh basil leaves

Directions:

1. Preheat the oven to 450F. In a large bowl, merge the tomatoes, garlic, 2tablespoons of oil, vinegar, salt and pepper. Spread the tomato mixture into a 9 x 13-inch pan and roast until the tomatoes begin to brown for about 30 minutes. Remove from the oven and set aside.

2. In a large saucepan, warmth the remaining tablespoon of oil over medium heat. Attach the onion, cover and cook until very soft for about10 minutes, stirring occasionally. Add the roasted tomatoes and stock, and then bring to a boil. Set the heat and simmer, uncovered, for 10 minutes. Remove from the heat, add the basil and season with salt and pepper. Merge the soup in the pot with an immersion blender or in a blender or food processor, as much as needed, and return to the pot. Reheat over medium heat if needed. To serve this cold soup, refrigerateit for at least 1 hour before serving.

Nutrition:

Calories: 222 Fat: 6g Carbohydrates: 43g Fiber: 5g Proteins: 3g

BUTTERNUT SQUASH

Preparation time: 10 minutes

Cooking time: 35 minutes

Servings: 6

Ingredients:

- 1 cup diced parsnips & 2 cups diced sweet potato
- 1 large sweet onion, peeled, diced
- 1 ½ cups diced carrots & 4 cups diced butternut squash
- 2 teaspoons minced garlic & ¼ teaspoon ground ginger
- ¼ teaspoon ground black pepper
- ½ teaspoon of sea salt & ¼ teaspoon ground allspice
- 1 teaspoon poultry seasoning & 1 teaspoon pumpkin pie spice
- ¼ teaspoon ground cinnamon
- 32 ounces vegetable stock
- 14 ounces coconut milk, unsweetened

Directions:

1. Take a large Dutch oven, put it over medium heat, add the onions, anddrizzle with 2 tablespoons of water and cook for 5 minutes until softened, sprinkling with more 2 tablespoons at a time as needed.

2. Then attach the garlic, cook for another minute, bring the heat to high,add the remaining shopping list: set aside milk, salt and black pepper and bring the soup to a boil.

3. Then change the heat to medium-low and simmer for 20 minutes untilthe vegetables are tender.

4. When done, blend the soup using a hand blender, then stir in thecoconut milk, set with salt and pepper and cook.

5. Serve immediately.

Nutrition:

Calories: 188.4 Fat: 7.7g Carbohydrates: 29.3g Proteins: 3.7g Fiber: 8.2g

Wonton Soup

Preparation time: 15 minutes

Cooking time: 10 minutes

Servings: 4

Ingredients:

For the Soup:
- 4 cups vegetable broth & 2 green onions, chopped

For the Wontons Filling:
- 1 cup chopped mushrooms
- ¼ cup walnuts, chopped
- 1 green onion, chopped & ½ inch of ginger, grated
- ½ teaspoon minced garlic & 1 tablespoon rice vinegar
- 2 teaspoons soy sauce
- 1 teaspoon brown sugar
- 20 Vegan Wonton Wrappers

Directions:

1. Prepare the filling of the wontons and for this, take a bowl, and put thewhole shopping list: in it, except the paper, and mix until well blended.

2. Place a wonton wrapper on the workspace, place 1 teaspoon of the prepared filling in the center, then brush some water around the edges,fold into a crescent shape, and seal the wraps by pinching the edges.

3. Take a large pot, put it on medium-high heat, add the broth and bring itto a boil.

4. Then pour in the prepared wontons, one at a time, and boil for 5minutes.

5. When cooked, garnish the soup with green onions and serve.

Nutrition:

Calories: 196.9 Fat: 4g Carbohydrates: 31g Proteins: 6.6g Fiber: 2.4g

POTATO AND KALE SOUP

Preparation time: 5 minutes

Cooking time: 15 minutes

Servings: 2

Ingredients:

- 1 small white onion, peeled, chopped
- 2 ½ cups cubed potatoes
- 2 cups leek, cut into rings
- ½ cup chopped carrots
- ½ cup chopped celery
- ½ teaspoon minced garlic
- ⅔ teaspoon salt
- ⅓ teaspoon ground black pepper
- 1 tablespoon olive oil
- 3 ½ cups vegetable broth
- 1 cup kale, cut into stripes
- Croutons, for serving

Directions:

1. Take a large pot, put it on medium heat, add the oil and, when it is hot,attach the onion and cook for 2 minutes until it is sautéed.

2. Set the garlic, cook for another minute, then add all the vegetables andcontinue cooking for 3 minutes.

3. Pour in the broth, cook for 15 minutes, then add the kale and cook for 2minutes until tender.

4. Flavor the soup with salt and black pepper, blend using a hand blenderuntil smooth, then top with croutons and serve.

Nutrition:

Calories: 337 Fat: 7g Carbohydrates: 62g Proteins: 10g Fiber: 8g

Ramen Soup

Preparation time: 10 minutes

Cooking time: 20 minutes

Servings: 2

Ingredients:

For the Mushrooms and Tofu:

- 2 cups sliced shiitake mushrooms
- 6 ounces tofu, extra-firm, drained, sliced
- 1 tablespoon olive oil
- 1 tablespoon soy sauce

For the Noodle Soup:
- 2 packs of dried ramen noodles
- 1 medium carrot, peeled, grated
- 1 inch of ginger, grated
- 1 teaspoon minced garlic
- ¾ cup baby spinach leaves
- 1 tablespoon olive oil
- 6 cups vegetable broth

For Garnish:
- Sesame seeds as needed
- Soy sauce as needed
- Sriracha sauce as needed

Directions:

1. Prepare the mushrooms and tofu and for this, put the tofu pieces in aplastic bag, add the soy sauce, seal the bag and turn it upside down until the tofu is coated.

2. Take a skillet, set it over medium heat, add the oil and, when hot, addthe tofu slices and cook for 5-10 minutes until crisp and golden on all sides, turning often and when cooked., set aside until needed.

3. Attach the mushrooms to the pan, cook for 8 minutes until

golden brown, pour the soy sauce from the tofu pieces and stir until coated.

4. In the meantime, prepare the noodle soup and for this, take a pot, put iton medium-high heat, attach the oil and when it is hot add the garlic and ginger and cook for 1 minute until not it is fragrant.

5. Then spill in the broth, bring the mixture to a boil, add the noodles andcook until tender.

6. Then mix the spinach into the noodle soup, remove the pot from theheat and distribute evenly between bowls.

7. Add the mushrooms and tofu along with the garnish and then serve.

Nutrition:

Calories: 647 Fat: 12g Carbohydrates: 106g Proteins: 28g Fiber: 6g

Vegetable and Barley Stew

Preparation time: 15 minutes

Cooking time: 20 minutes

Servings: 6

Ingredients:

- 2 or 3 parsnips, peeled and chopped
- 2 cups chopped peeled sweet potato, russet potato, winter squash, or pumpkin
- 1 large yellow onion, chopped
- 1 cup pearl barley
- 1 (28-ounce) can diced tomatoes
- 4 cups water or unsalted vegetable broth
- 2 to 3 teaspoons dried mixed herbs or 1 teaspoon dried basil plus 1 teaspoon dried oregano
- Salt
- Freshly ground black pepper

Directions:

1. In your electric pressure cooker, combine the parsnips, sweet potato,onion, and barley, tomatoes with their juice, water, and herbs.

2. High pressure for 20 minutes. Secure the lid, then select High pressureand set the time to 20 minutes.

3. Pressure release. Once the

4. Cooking time is finished, quickly release thepressure. Once all pressure has been released, carefully unlock and remove the lid. Taste and season with salt and pepper.

Nutrition:

Calories: 300 Proteins: 9g Fat: 2g Carbohydrates: 16g Fiber: 14g

VEGAN PHO

Preparation time: 5 minutes

Cooking time: 15 minutes

Servings: 6

Ingredients:

- 1 package of wide rice noodles, cooked
- 1 medium white onion, peeled, quartered
- 2 teaspoons minced garlic
- 1 inch of ginger, sliced into coins
- 8 cups vegetable broth
- 3 whole cloves
- 2 tablespoons soy sauce
- 3 whole star anise
- 1 cinnamon stick
- 3 cups of water

For Toppings:

- Basil as needed for topping
- Chopped green onions as needed for topping
- Mung beans as needed for topping
- Hot sauce as needed for topping
- Lime wedges for serving

Directions:

1. Take a large pot, put it on medium-high heat, add the whole ShoppingList: for the soup, except the soy sauce and broth, and bring to a boil.

2. Then change the heat to medium-low, simmer the soup for 30 minutesand then add the soy sauce.

3. When finished, spread the cooked noodles into bowls, add the soup,then garnish and serve.

Nutrition:

Calories: 31 Fat: 0g Carbohydrates: 7g Proteins: 0g Fiber: 2g

GARDEN VEGETABLE STEW

Preparation time: 6 minutes

Cooking time: 60 minutes

Servings: 4

Ingredients:

- 2 tablespoons extra-virgin olive oil
- 1 medium red onion, chopped
- 1 medium carrot
- ½ cup dry white wine
- 3 medium new potatoes, unpeeled and cut into 1-inch pieces
- 1 medium red bell pepper
- 1½ cups vegetable broth
- 2 medium zucchinis, trimmed, halved lengthwise, and cut into ½-inch slices
- 1 medium yellow summer squash, trimmed, halved lengthwise, and cut into ½-inch slices
- 1 pound ripe plum tomatoes, chopped
- Salt and freshly ground black pepper
- 2 cups fresh corn kernels
- 1 cup fresh peas
- ¼ cup fresh basil
- ¼ cup chopped fresh parsley
- 1 tbsp. minced fresh savory or 1 teaspoon dried

Directions:

1. In a large saucepan, warmth the oil over medium heat. Attach the onion and carrot, cover and cook until softened for 7 minutes. Attach the wineand cook, uncovered, for 5 minutes. Stir in the potatoes, pepper and broth, then bring to a boil. Lower the heat to medium and stew for 15 minutes.

2. Add the courgette, yellow squash and tomatoes. Flavor with salt andblack pepper, cover and simmer until vegetables are tender for 20-30minutes.

3. Finish and serve

4. Mix the corn, peas, basil, parsley and savory. Taste, adjusting the seasonings if necessary. Stew to mix the flavors for about 10 moreminutes. Serve immediately.

Nutrition:

Calories: 166 Fat: 8g Carbohydrates: 24g Fiber: 6.5g Proteins: 9g

Moroccan Vegetable Stew

Preparation time: 5 minutes

Cooking time: 35 minutes

Servings: 4

Ingredients:

- 1 tablespoon extra-virgin olive oil
- 2 medium yellow onions, chopped
- 2 medium carrots
- ½ teaspoon ground cumin
- ½ teaspoon ground cinnamon or allspice
- ½ teaspoon ground ginger
- ½ teaspoon sweet or smoked paprika
- ½ teaspoon saffron or turmeric
- 1 (14.5-ounce) can diced tomatoes, undrained
- 8 ounces green beans
- 2 cups peeled, seeded, and diced winter squash
- 1 large russet or other baking potato, peeled and cut into ½-inch dice
- 1½ cups vegetable broth
- 1½ cups cooked or 1 can chickpeas, drained and rinsed
- ¾ cup frozen peas
- ½ cup pitted dried plums (prunes)
- 1 teaspoon lemon zest
- Salt and freshly ground black pepper
- ½ cup pitted green olives
- 1 tablespoon minced fresh cilantro or parsley, for garnish
- ½ cup toasted slivered almonds, for garnish

Directions:

1. In a large saucepan, warmth the oil over medium heat. Attach the onions and carrots, cover and cook for 5 minutes. Incorporate the cumin, cinnamon, ginger, paprika and saffron. Cook uncovered and mix for 30 seconds. Add the tomatoes, green beans, squash, potato andbroth and bring to a boil. Lower

the heat, secure and simmer until the vegetables are tender for about 20 minutes.

2. Finish and serve

3. Add the chickpeas, peas, prunes and lemon zest. Season with salt and pepper. Incorporate the olives and simmer, uncovered, until the flavorshave blended for about 10 minutes. Sprinkle it with cilantro and almonds, and then serve immediately.

Nutrition:

Calories: 139 Fat: 1.4g Carbohydrates: 28g Fiber: 11g Proteins: 5g

Matzo Ball Soup

Preparation time: 5 minutes

Cooking time: 45 minutes

Servings: 4

Ingredients:

- 1 tablespoon extra-virgin olive oil
- 1 small onion, finely chopped
- 1 medium carrot, chopped
- 1 celery rib, chopped
- 3 green onions, chopped
- 6 cups vegetable broth, homemade or store-bought, or water
- 2 tablespoons minced fresh parsley
- 1 teaspoon fresh or dried dill weed
- ½ teaspoon salt, or more if needed
- ¼ teaspoon freshly ground black pepper
- Matzo Balls (recipe follows)

Directions:

1. In a large saucepan, set the oil over medium heat. Add the onion, carrotand celery. Secure and cook until softened for about 5 minutes. Add thegreen onions and cook for 3 minutes more. Incorporate the broth, parsley, dill, salt and pepper. Set to a boil, and then lower the heat to low and simmer, uncovered, until the vegetables are tender for about 30minutes.

2. Finish and serve

3. When ready to serve, place three matzo balls in each bowl and pour thesoup over them. Serve immediately.

Nutrition:

Calories: 420 Fat: 15.2g Carbohydrates: 64.3g Proteins: 11.6g

White Bean and Broccoli Salad

Preparation time: 10 minutes

Cooking time: 15 minutes

Servings: 4-6

Ingredients:

- 1 pound Yukon Gold potatoes, peel off and cut into 1-inch chunks
- 3 cups broccoli florets
- 1½ cups cooked or 15.5-ounce can cannellini or other white beans, drained and rinsed
- ¼ cup kalamata olives
- ½ cup walnut pieces
- 2 garlic cloves, finely minced
- ½ cup chopped fresh parsley
- ¼ cup walnut oil
- ¼ cup extra-virgin olive oil
- ¼ cup white wine vinegar
- ½ teaspoon salt (optional)
- ¼ teaspoon crushed red pepper

Directions:

1. Steam the potatoes until almost tender for about 10 minutes. Steam thebroccoli until tender for about 5 minutes. Drain the potatoes and broccoli and put them in a large bowl. Add the beans, olives and ¼ cupof walnuts and set aside.

2. In a blender or food processor, merge the remaining ¼ cup of walnutswith the garlic and blend until well-chopped. Add the parsley, walnutoil, olive oil, vinegar, salt, sugar and chopped chili and blend until smooth. Spill the dressing over the salad, stirring gently to combine, and then serve.

Nutrition:

Calories: 294 Fat: 6g Carbohydrates: 19.5g Fiber: 12g Proteins: 22.5g

Chinese Black Bean Chili

Preparation time: 15 minutes

Cooking time: 0 minutes

Servings: 4

Ingredients:

- 1 tablespoon extra-virgin olive oil
- 1 medium yellow onion, finely chopped
- 2 medium carrots, finely chopped
- 1 teaspoon grated fresh ginger
- 2 tablespoons chili powder
- 1 teaspoon brown sugar
- 1 (28-ounce) can diced tomatoes, undrained
- ½ cup Chinese black bean sauce
- ¾ cup water
- ½ cans black beans, drained and rinsed
- Salt and freshly ground black pepper
- 2 tablespoons minced green onion, for garnish

Directions:

1. In a large saucepan, set the oil over medium heat. Add the onion andcarrot. Cover and cook until softened for about 10 minutes.

2. Stir in the ginger, chili powder and sugar. Add the tomatoes, black beansauce and water. Incorporate the black beans and season with salt and pepper.

3. Set to a boil, and then lower the heat to medium and simmer, covered,until the vegetables are tender for about 30 minutes.

4. Simmer for about 10 minutes more. Serve immediately garnished withgreen onion.

Nutrition:

Calories: 302 Fat: 22g Carbohydrates: 5g Proteins: 34g

Coconut Rice

Preparation time: 10 minutes

Cooking time: 25 minutes

Servings: 7

Ingredients:

- 2 ½ cups white rice
- ⅛ teaspoon salt
- 40 ounces coconut milk, unsweetened

Directions:

1. Take a large saucepan; put it on medium heat, add the whole ShoppingList: inside and mix until combined.

2. Set the mixture to a boil, then bring the heat to medium-low and simmer the rice for 25 minutes until tender and all liquid is absorbed.

3. Serve immediately.

Nutrition:

Calories: 535 Fat: 33.2g Carbohydrates: 57g Proteins: 8.1g Fiber: 2.1g

BAKED BEANS

Preparation time: 5 minutes

Cooking time: 45 minutes

Servings: 4

Ingredients:

- 1 tablespoon extra-virgin olive oil
- 1 medium yellow onion, minced
- 3 garlic cloves, minced
- 1 (14.5-ounce) can crushed tomatoes
- ½ cup pure maple syrup & 2 tablespoons blackstrap molasses
- 1 tablespoon soy sauce
- 1½ teaspoons dry mustard & ¼ teaspoon ground cayenne
- Salt and freshly ground black pepper
- 3 cups cooked Great Northern beans

Directions:

1. Preheat the oven to 350F.

2. Lightly grease a 2-quart saucepan and set aside.

3. In a large saucepan, warmth the oil over medium heat. Add the onionand garlic. Secure and cook until softened for about 5 minutes.

4. Stir in the tomatoes, maple syrup, molasses, soy sauce, mustard, andcayenne pepper and set to a boil.

5. Set the heat to low and stew, unsealed, until slightly reduced for about10 minutes. Season with salt and pepper.

6. Put the beans in the prepared saucepan. Add the sauce, stirring to mixand coat the beans. Cover and cook until hot and bubbly for about 30minutes. Serve immediately

Nutrition:

Calories: 398 Carbohydrates: 55.6g Proteins: 17.8g Fat: 11.8g

LEMONY QUINOA

Preparation time: 10 minutes

Cooking time: 0 minute

Servings: 6

Ingredients:

- 1 cup quinoa, cooked
- ¼ of medium red onion, peeled, chopped
- 1 bunch of parsley, chopped
- 2 stalks of celery, chopped
- ¼ teaspoon of sea salt
- ¼ teaspoon cayenne pepper
- ½ teaspoon ground cumin
- ¼ cup lemon juice
- ¼ cup pine nuts, toasted

Directions:

1. Take a large bowl, place all the Shopping List: in it, and stir untilcombined.

2. Serve straight away.

Nutrition:

Calories: 147 Fat: 4.8g Carbohydrates: 21.4g Proteins: 6g Fiber: 3g

VEGAN CURRIED RICE

Preparation time: 5 minutes

Cooking time: 25 minutes

Servings: 4

Ingredients:

- 1 cup white rice
- 1 tablespoon minced garlic
- 1 tablespoon ground curry powder
- ⅓ teaspoon ground black pepper
- 1 tablespoon red chili powder
- 1 tablespoon ground cumin
- 2 tablespoons olive oil
- 1 tablespoon soy sauce
- 1 cup vegetable broth

Directions:

1. Take a saucepan, put it on low heat, add the oil and when it is hotattach the garlic and cook for 3 minutes.

2. Then add all the spices, cook for 1 minute until fragrant, pour in thebroth and bring the heat to a high level.

3. Stir in the soy sauce, bring the mixture to a boil, add the rice, stir until combined, then turn the heat to low and simmer for 20 minutes until therice is tender and all the liquid is absorbed.

4. Serve immediately.

Nutrition:

Calories: 262 Fat: 8g Carbohydrates: 43g Proteins: 5g Fiber: 2g

Spicy Cabbage Salad

Preparation time: 5 minutes

Cooking time: 5 minutes

Servings: 4

Ingredients:

- 1 head Napa cabbage
- 1 cup carrots
- ½ cup green onions
- 1 bell pepper & ½ cup cilantro
- 1 jalapeño chili pepper & ½ cup sunflower seeds
- ½ cup almond butter
- ¼ cup canned coconut milk
- ¼ cup apple cider vinegar
- ¼ cup onion & 2 tbsp. white miso paste
- 2 tbsp. maple syrup & 1 tbsp. red curry paste
- 3 garlic cloves
- ½-inch piece ginger

Directions:

1. Cut the end of the cabbage, halve and core it, then cut thinly. Shred carrots thinly slice green onions and pepper, chop cilantro and jalapeño. Combine all in a large bowl with sunflower seeds. Set aside.

2. Roughly chop onion.

3. Make the sauce by blending the almond butter, coconut milk, vinegar, onion, miso, maple syrup, curry paste, garlic, and ginger. Blend until smooth and mixed. If needed, attach water to thin it out.

4. Pour the dressing over the veggie mix and toss to coat.\

Nutrition:

Calories: 301 Carbohydrates: 21g Fat: 17g Proteins: 8g

Wholesome Farm Salad

Preparation time: 15 minutes

Cooking time: 4 hours

Servings: 5

Ingredients:

- ½ cup hulled barley
- 2 beetroots
- 2 tbsp. sunflower seeds
- 6 cups romaine lettuce
- ½ cup scallions
- ½ cup coriander
- 2 tbsp. raisins
- ½ cup orange juice
- 1 tbsp. lemon juice
- Black pepper
- Himalayan pink salt

Directions:

1. In a large bowl, cover barley with water, then leave to soak for at least3 hours.

2. Drain the barley water and add barley to a pot over high heat. Attach 2cups of water and boil for 5 to 7 minutes, then turn heat to low and cover the pot. Simmer for 25 minutes or until the barley is tender but not soft. Drain and set aside to cool to room temperature.

3. Scrub the outside of the beets then cut each into quarters.

4. Put the beets in a medium pan and add water until it covers the beets.Set to a boil, then simmer partially covered. Stew for 30 minutes or until the beets are tender. Drain. Peel off the beets while they are stillwarm and cut them into bite-size pieces. Set aside.

5. Toast the sunflower seeds over medium high heat, stirring

every sooften, for 5 minutes or until barely toasted. Let cool on a plate.

6. Chop romaine, green onion, and cilantro.

7. In a large bowl, attach the barley and beets. Add romaine, green onions,cilantro, raisins, orange juice, lemon juice, a sprinkle of pepper, and a pinch of salt. Toss gently then sprinkle the toasted sunflower seeds overthe salad.

Nutrition:

Calories: 245 Fat: 18.9g Carbohydrate: 15.9g Proteins: 6.4g

Spicy Chickpea Crunch

Preparation time: 5 minutes

Cooking time: 0 minutes

Servings: 2

Ingredients:

- 1 garlic clove
- 1 tbsp. sesame oil
- 2 tbsp. rice vinegar
- ½ tsp. hot sauce & 2 tbsp. tamari
- 1 tsp. maple syrup & 2 tsp. sesame seeds
- 2 cups spinach
- 1 can chickpeas
- 2 stalks celery
- 2 carrots & ½ cucumber
- 2 green onions & 1 ripe avocado
- 4 tbsp. walnuts

Directions:

1. Mince garlic and whisk with the oil, vinegar, hot sauce, tamari, maple syrup, and sesame seeds until combined. Refrigerate until ready to serve.

2. Evenly divide the spinach between two serving bowls.

3. Drain and rinse the chickpeas, then half it between the bowls.

4. Thinly slice the celery, carrots, cucumber, green onions, and chop the avocado. Divide evenly between each bowl.

5. Thinly slice or chop walnuts and sprinkle half over each bowl. Use a measuring spoon to pour 1 tbsp. of the previously prepared dressing into each bowl and serve promptly.

Nutrition:

Calories: 384 Fat: 14g Carbohydrates: 58g Fiber: 6g Proteins: 11g

EASY ITALIAN BOWL

Preparation time: 15 minutes

Cooking time: 5 minutes

Servings: 5

Ingredients:

- 1 red onion
- 1 cup basil
- 12 ounces wheat spiral pasta
- 1 bag assorted frozen vegetables
- 1 cup balsamic vinaigrette
- Salt
- Pepper

Directions:

1. Finely dice onion and basil.

2. Boil water and cook the pasta. During the last 5 minutes of cooking,attach frozen vegetables to the pot. Drain the pasta and vegetables. Rinse under cold water until cool.

3. Move mixture to a large bowl. Add the onion, vinaigrette, and basil. Gently mix to coat. Add a pinch of salt and pepper. Can be served coldor room-temperature.

Nutrition:

Calories: 150 Fat: 7.3g Fiber: 6.1g Carbohydrates: 18g Proteins: 3.7g

Dinner

SWEET AND SOUR TEMPEH

Preparation time: 10 minutes

Cooking time: 8 minutes

Servings: 4

Ingredients:

- 1 cup pineapple juice
- 1 tablespoon unseasoned rice vinegar
- 1 tablespoon soy sauce
- 1 tablespoon cornstarch
- 2 tablespoons coconut oil
- 1-pound tempeh, cut into thin strips
- 6 green onions
- 1 green bell pepper, diced
- 4 garlic cloves, minced
- 2 cups prepared brown or white rice

Directions:

1. Blend pineapple juice, rice vinegar, soy sauce, and cornstarch and setaside.

2. In a wok or large sauté pan, warmth the coconut oil over medium-highheat until it shimmers. Add the tempeh, green onions, and bell pepper,and cook until vegetables soften about 5 minutes.

3. Cook garlic. Set in sauce and cook until it thickens. Serve over rice.

Nutrition:

Calories: 244 Fat: 2g Proteins: 11g Carbohydrates: 50g Fiber: 10g

FRIED SEITAN FINGERS

Preparation time: 15 minutes

Cooking time: 10 minutes

Servings: 4

Ingredients:

- 1 cup all-purpose flour
- 1 teaspoon garlic powder
- 1 teaspoon onion powder
- Pinch of cayenne pepper
- 1 teaspoon dried thyme
- ½ teaspoon sea salt
- ½ teaspoon freshly ground black pepper
- 1 cup soy milk
- 1 tablespoon lemon juice
- 2 tablespoons baking powder
- 2 tablespoons olive oil
- 8 ounces Seitan

Directions:

1. In a shallow dish, incorporate the flour, garlic powder, onion powder, cayenne, thyme, salt, and black pepper, whisking to mix thoroughly. Inanother shallow dish, whisk together the soy milk, lemon juice, and baking powder.

2. In a sauté pan, cook the olive oil over medium-high heat. Set each pieceof seitan in the flour mixture, tapping off any excess flour. Next, dip the seitan in the soymilk mixture and then back into the flour mixture.

3. Fry for 4 minutes per side. Blot on paper towels before serving.

Nutrition:

Calories: 388 Fat: 19g Carbohydrates: 45g Fiber: 12g Sugar: 13g

CRUSTY GRILLED CORN

Preparation time: 10 minutes

Cooking time: 15 minutes

Servings: 4

Ingredients:

- 2 corn cobs
- ⅓ cup Vegenaise
- 1 small handful cilantro
- ½ cup breadcrumbs
- 1 teaspoon lemon juice

Directions:

1. Preheat the gas grill on high heat.
2. Add corn grill to the grill and continue grilling until it turns golden-brown on all sides.
3. Mix the Vegenaise, cilantro, breadcrumbs, and lemon juice in a bowl.
4. Add grilled corn cobs to the crumbs mixture.
5. Toss well then serve.

Nutrition:

Calories: 253 Fat: 13g Proteins: 31g Fiber: 0g Carbohydrates: 3g

Grilled Carrots with Chickpea Salad

Preparation time: 10 minutes.

Cooking time: 5 minutes.

Servings: 8

Ingredients:

- 8 large carrots & 1 tablespoon oil
- 1(½) teaspoon salt & 1 teaspoon dried oregano
- 1 teaspoon dried thyme
- 2 teaspoons paprika powder
- 1(½) tablespoon soy sauce
- ½ cup of water

Chickpea salad:
- 14 ounces canned chickpeas
- 3 medium pickles
- 1 small onion & A big handful of lettuce
- 1 teaspoon apple cider vinegar
- ½ teaspoon dried oregano & ½ teaspoon salt
- Ground black pepper to taste
- ½ cup vegan cream

Directions:

1. Toss the carrots with all the ingredients in a bowl.

2. Thread one carrot on a stick and place it on a plate.

3. Preheat the grill over high heat.

4. Grill the carrots for 2 minutes per side on the grill.

5. Toss the ingredients for the salad in a large salad bowl.

6. Slice grilled carrots and add them on top of the salad.

7. Serve fresh.

Nutrition:

Calories: 661 Fat: 68g Carbohydrates: 7g Fiber: 2g Proteins: 4g

GRILLED AVOCADO GUACAMOLE

Preparation time: 10 minutes

Cooking time: 22 minutes

Servings: 4

Ingredients:

- ½ teaspoon olive oil
- 1 lime, halved
- ½ onion, halved
- 1 serrano chili, halved, stemmed, and seeded
- 3 Haas avocados, skin on
- 2-3 tablespoons fresh cilantro, chopped
- ½ teaspoon smoked salt

Directions:

1. Preheat the grill over medium heat.

2. Brush the grilling grates with olive oil and place chili, onion, and limeon them.

3. Grill the onion for 10 minutes, chili for 5 minutes, and lime for 2minutes.

4. Transfer the veggies to a large bowl.

5. Now cut the avocados in half and grill them for 5 minutes.

6. Mash the flesh of the grilled avocado in a bowl.

7. Chop the other grilled veggies and add them to the avocado mash.

8. Stir in the remaining ingredients and merge well. Serve.

Nutrition:

Calories: 165 Fat: 17g Carbohydrates: 4g Fiber: 1g Proteins: 1g

Spinach and Dill Pasta Salad

Preparation time: 5 minutes

Cooking time: 0 minutes

Servings: 4

Ingredients:

For the salad:

- 3 cups cooked whole-wheat fusilli
- 2 cups cherry tomatoes, halved
- ½ cup vegan cheese, shredded
- 4 cups spinach, chopped
- 2 cups edamame, thawed
- 1 large red onion, finely chopped

For the dressing:

- 2 tablespoons white wine vinegar
- ½ teaspoon dried dill
- 2 tablespoons extra-virgin olive oil
- Salt to taste
- Pepper to taste

Directions:

1. To make the dressing: Attach all the ingredients for dressing into abowl and whisk well. Set aside for a while for the flavors to set in.

2. To make the salad: Add all the ingredients of the salad to a bowl. Toss well. Drizzle dressing on top. Toss well. Divide into 4 plates and serve.

Nutrition:

Calories: 684 Fat: 33.6g Carbohydrate: 69.5g

Italian Veggie Salad

Preparation time: 10 minutes

Cooking time: 0 minutes

Servings: 8

Ingredients:

For the salad:

- 1 cup fresh baby carrots, quartered lengthwise
- 1 celery rib, sliced
- 3 large mushrooms, thinly sliced
- 1 cup cauliflower florets, bite-sized, blanched
- 1 cup broccoli florets, blanched
- 1 cup thinly sliced radish
- 4–5 ounces hearts of romaine salad mix to serve
- For the dressing:
- ½ package Italian salad dressing mix
- 3 tablespoons white vinegar
- 3 tablespoons water
- 3 tablespoons olive oil
- 3-4 pepperoncini, chopped

Directions:

1. To make the salad: Add all the ingredients of the salad except hearts ofromaine to a bowl and toss.

2. To make the dressing: Attach all the ingredients of the dressing in a small bowl. Whisk well. Pour dressing over salad and toss well. Refrigerate for a couple of hours. Place romaine in a large bowl. Placethe chilled salad over it and serve.

Nutrition:

Calories: 84 Fat: 6.7g Carbohydrate: 5g

Spinach and Mashed Tofu Salad

Preparation time: 20 minutes

Cooking time: 0 minutes

Servings: 4

Ingredients:

- 2(8-ounces) blocks firm tofu, drained
- 4 cups baby spinach leaves
- 4 tablespoons cashew butter
- 1(½) tablespoon soy sauce
- 1 tablespoon ginger, chopped
- 1 teaspoon red miso paste
- 2 tablespoons sesame seeds
- 1 teaspoon organic orange zest
- 1 teaspoon nori flakes
- 2 tablespoons water

Directions:

1. In a bowl, merge the mashed tofu with the spinach leaves.

2. Merge the remaining ingredients in another small bowl and, if desired,add the optional water for a smoother dressing.

3. Spill this dressing over the mashed tofu and spinach leaves.

4. Set the bowl to the fridge and allow the salad to chill. Enjoy!

Nutrition:

Calories: 623 Fat: 30.5g Carbohydrate: 48g

SUPER SUMMER SALAD

Preparation time: 10 minutes.

Cooking time: 0 minutes.

Servings: 2

Ingredients:

Dressing:

- 1 tablespoon olive oil
- ¼ cup chopped basil
- 1 teaspoon lemon juice
- ¼ teaspoon salt & 1 medium avocado, halved, diced
- ¼ cup water Salad:& ¼ cup dry chickpeas
- ¼ cup dry red kidney beans & 4 cups raw kale, shredded
- 2 cups Brussels sprouts, shredded
- 2 radishes, thinly sliced & 1 tablespoon walnuts, chopped
- 1 teaspoon flax seeds & Salt and pepper to taste

Directions:

1. Prepare the chickpeas and kidney beans according to the method. Soak the flaxseeds according to the method and then drain excesswater.

2. Attach the olive oil, basil, lemon juice, salt, and half of the avocado to afood processor or blender, and pulse at low speed. Set the dressing to a small bowl and set it aside.

3. Combine the kale, Brussels sprouts, cooked chickpeas, kidney beans,radishes, walnuts, and the remaining avocado in a large bowl and mix thoroughly.

4. Store the mixture, or serve with the dressing and flaxseeds, and enjoy!

Nutrition:

Calories: 266 Fat: 26.6g Carbohydrates: 8.8g Fiber: 6.8g Proteins: 2g

ROASTED ALMOND PROTEIN SALAD

Preparation time: 30 minutes

Cooking time: 0 minutes

Servings: 4

Ingredients:

- ½ cup dry quinoa
- ½ cup dry navy beans
- ½ cup dry chickpeas
- ½ cup raw whole almonds
- 1 teaspoon extra-virgin olive oil
- ½ teaspoon salt
- ½ teaspoon paprika
- ½ teaspoon cayenne
- Dash of chili powder
- 4 cups spinach, fresh or frozen
- ¼ cup purple onion, chopped

Directions:

1. Prepare the quinoa according to the recipe. Store in the fridge for now.Prepare the beans according to the method. Store in the fridge for now.Set the almonds, olive oil, salt, and spices in a large bowl, and stir untilthe ingredients are evenly coated.

2. Set a skillet over medium-high heat and transfer the almond mixture tothe heated skillet.

3. Roast while stirring. Stir frequently to prevent burning.

4. Set off the heat and toss the cooked and chilled quinoa and beans, onions, spinach, or mixed greens in the skillet. Stir well and set theroasted almond salad to a bowl.

5. Enjoy!

Nutrition:

Calories: 347 Fat: 10.5g Carbohydrate: 49.2g Fiber: 14.7g

Lentil, Lemon and Mushroom Salad

Preparation time: 10 minutes

Cooking time: 10-15 minutes

Servings: 2

Ingredients:

- ½ cup dry lentils of choice
- 2 cups vegetable broth
- 3 cups mushrooms, thickly sliced
- 1 cup sweet or purple onion, chopped
- 4 teaspoons extra-virgin olive oil
- 2 tablespoons garlic powder
- ¼ teaspoon chili flakes
- 1 tablespoon lemon juice
- 2 tablespoons cilantro, chopped
- ½ cup arugula
- ¼ teaspoon salt
- ¼ teaspoon pepper

Directions:

1. Sprout the lentils according to the method. (Don't cook them).

2. Place the vegetable stock in a deep saucepan and bring it to a boil.

3. Add the lentils to the boiling broth, cover the pan, and cook for about 5minutes over low heat until the lentils are a bit tender.

4. Remove the pan from heat and drain the excess water.

5. Set a frying pan over high heat and attach 2 tablespoons of olive oil.

6. Add the onions, garlic, and chili flakes, and cook until the onions arealmost translucent, around 5 to 10 minutes while stirring.

7. Attach the mushrooms to the frying pan and mix in thoroughly.

Continue cooking until the onions are completely translucent and themushrooms have softened; remove the pan from the heat.

8. Mix the lentils, onions, mushrooms, and garlic in a large bowl.

9. Attach the lemon juice and the remaining olive oil. Toss or stir tocombine everything thoroughly.

10. Serve the mushroom/onion mixture over some arugula in a bowl, adding salt and pepper to taste, or store and enjoy later!

Nutrition:

Calories: 365 Fat: 11.7g Carbohydrates: 45.2g Proteins: 22.8g

Sweet Potato and Black Bean Protein Salad

Preparation time: 15 minutes.

Cooking time: 400 minutes.

Servings: 2

Ingredients:

- 1 cup dry black beans
- 4 cups of spinach
- 1 medium sweet potato
- 1 cup purple onion, chopped
- 2 tablespoons olive oil
- 2 tablespoons lime juice
- 1 tablespoon minced garlic
- ½ tablespoon chili powder
- ¼ teaspoon cayenne
- ¼ cup parsley
- ¼ teaspoons salt
- ¼ teaspoons pepper

Directions:

1. Prepare the black beans according to the method.

2. Preheat the oven to 400F.

3. Cut the sweet potato into ¼-inch cubes and put these in a medium-sizedbowl. Add the onions, 1 tablespoon of olive oil, and salt to taste.

4. Toss the ingredients until the sweet potatoes and onions are completelycoated.

5. Transfer the ingredients to a baking sheet lined with parchment paperand spread them out in a single layer.

6. Bring the baking sheet in the oven and roast until the sweet potatoesstart to turn brown and crispy, around 40 minutes.

7. Meanwhile, combine the remaining olive oil, lime juice, garlic,

chilipowder, and cayenne thoroughly in a large bowl, until no lumps remain.

8. Detach the sweet potatoes and onions from the oven and transfer themto the large bowl.

9. Add the cooked black beans, parsley, and a pinch of salt.

10. Toss everything until well combined.

11. Then mix in the spinach and serve in desired portions with additionalsalt and pepper.

12. Store or enjoy!

Nutrition:

Calories: 558 Fat: 6.2g Carbohydrate: 84g Fiber: 20.4g

Lentil Radish Salad

Preparation time: 15 minutes

Cooking time: 0 minutes

Servings: 3

Ingredients:

Dressing:
- 1 tablespoon extra-virgin olive oil
- 1 tablespoon lemon juice
- 1 tablespoon maple syrup
- 1 tablespoon water
- ½ tablespoon sesame oil
- 1 tablespoon miso paste, yellow or white
- ¼ teaspoon salt
- ¼ teaspoons
- Pepper Salad:
- ½ cup dry chickpeas
- ¼ cup dry green
- 1(14-ounce) pack of silken tofu
- 5 cups mixed greens, fresh or frozen
- 2 radishes, thinly sliced
- ½ cup cherry tomatoes, halved
- ¼ cup roasted sesame seeds

Directions:

1. Prepare the chickpeas according to the method.

2. Prepare the lentils according to the method.

3. Set all the ingredients for the dressing in a blender or food processor.Mix on low until smooth, while adding water until it reaches the desired consistency.

4. Add salt, pepper (to taste), and optionally more water to the dressing;set aside.

5. Cut the tofu into bite-sized cubes.

6. Combine the mixed greens, tofu, lentils, chickpeas, radishes, andtomatoes in a large bowl.

7. Add the dressing and mix everything until it is coated evenly.

8. Top with the optional roasted sesame seeds, if desired.

9. Refrigerate before serving and enjoy, or store for later!

Nutrition:

Calories: 621 Fat: 19.6g Carbohydrates: 82.7g Fiber: 26.1g

Jicama and Spinach Salad Recipe

Preparation time: 10 minutes

Cooking time: 20 minutes

Servings: 4

Ingredients:

Salad:

- 10 ounces baby spinach, washed and dried
- 16 grape or cherry tomatoes
- 1 jicama
- Green or Kalamata olives, chopped
- 8 teaspoons walnuts, chopped
- 1 teaspoon raw or roasted sunflower seeds

Dressing:

- 1 heaping tablespoon Dijon mustard
- Dash cayenne pepper to taste
- 2 tablespoons maple syrup
- 2 garlic cloves, minced
- 1 to 2 tablespoons water
- ¼ teaspoons sea salt

Directions:

1. For the salad: Divide the baby spinach onto 4 salad plates. Set each serving with ¼ of the jicama, ¼ of the chopped olives, and 4 tomatoes.Sprinkle 1 teaspoon of the sunflower seeds and 2 teaspoons of the walnuts.

2. For the dressing: In a small mixing bowl, whisk all the ingredients together until emulsified. Check the taste and add more maple syrup forsweetness. Drizzle 1(½) tablespoon of the dressing over each salad and serve.

Nutrition:

Calories: 196 Fat: 2g Proteins: 7g Carbohydrates: 28g Fiber: 12g

HIGH-PROTEIN SALAD

Preparation time: 5 minutes.

Cooking time: 0 minutes.

Servings: 4 **Ingredients:**

Salad:

- 1(15-ounces) can green kidney beans
- 4 tablespoons capers
- 4 handfuls arugula
- 4(15-ounces) can lentils

Dressing:

- 1 tablespoon caper brine
- 1 tablespoon tamari
- 1 tablespoon balsamic vinegar
- 2 tablespoons peanut butter
- 2 tablespoons hot sauce
- 1 tablespoon tahini

Directions:

1. For the dressing: In a bowl, spill together all the ingredients until theycome together to form a smooth dressing.

2. For the salad: Mix the beans, arugula, capers, and lentils. Top with thedressing and serve.

Nutrition:

Calories: 205 Fat: 2g Proteins: 13g Carbohydrates: 31g Fiber: 17g

MUSSELS IN RED WINE SAUCE

Preparation time: 5 minutes

Cooking time: 3 minutes

Servings: 2

Ingredients:

- 800g mussels
- 2 x 400g tins of chopped tomatoes
- 25g butter
- 1 fresh chives, chopped
- 1 fresh parsley, chopped
- 1 bird's-eye chili, finely chopped
- 4 cloves of garlic, crushed
- 400 ml red wine
- Juice of 1 lemon

Directions:

1. Wash the mussels, remove their beards, and set them aside. Warmth thebutter in a large saucepan and add in the red wine. Reduce the heat and add the parsley, chives, chili, and garlic whilst stirring. Add in the tomatoes, lemon juice, and mussels. Cover the saucepan and cook for 2-3 minutes.

2. Remove the saucepan from the heat and take out any mussels which haven't opened and discard them. Serve and eat immediately.

Nutrition:

Calories: 364 Carbohydrates: 3.3g Fat: 4.9g Proteins: 8g

ROAST BALSAMIC VEGETABLES

Preparation time: 10 minutes

Cooking time: 45 minutes

Servings: 4

Ingredients:

- 4 tomatoes, chopped
- 2 red onions, chopped
- 3 sweet potatoes, peeled and chopped
- 100g red chicory (or if unavailable, use yellow)
- 100g kale, finely chopped
- 300g potatoes, peeled and chopped
- 5 stalks of celery, chopped
- 1 bird's-eye chili, de-seeded and finely chopped
- 2g fresh parsley, chopped
- 2g fresh coriander (cilantro) chopped
- 3 teaspoons olive oil
- 2 teaspoons balsamic vinegar
- 1 teaspoon mustard
- Sea salt
- Freshly ground black pepper

Directions:

1. Place the olive oil, balsamic, mustard, parsley, and coriander (cilantro)into a bowl and mix well.

2. Toss all the remaining ingredients into the dressing and season with saltand pepper.

3. Transfer the vegetables to an ovenproof dish and cook in the oven at200C/400F for 45 minutes.

Nutrition:

Calories: 98 Fiber: 2g Proteins: 3g Carbohydrates: 3.1g

Vegan Caesar Salad

Preparation time: 20 minutes

Cooking time: 1 hours 20 minutes

Servings: 4

Ingredients:

- 1 15-oz can chickpeas
- ½ tsp. grated lemon zest
- 1 tbsp. olive oil
- Salt and pepper
- ¼ c. olive oil
- 1 tsp. grated lemon zest plus ⅓cup lemon juice
- ¼ c. tahini
- 2 tsp. capers plus 1 tsp caper brine
- 1 small clove garlic, finely grated
- 1 tbsp. nutritional yeast
- 1 tbsp. Dijon mustard
- 3 tbsp. olive oil
- 4 thick slices bread
- 2 small red onions, cut into thick rounds
- 2 heads gem lettuce or romaine hearts, leaves separated
- 2 bunches small radishes
- 1 clove garlic, cut in half

Directions:

Crispy Chickpeas:

1. Preheat the oven to 425 degrees Fahrenheit. Rinse the chickpeas andpat them dry with paper towels, removing any loose skins.

2. Toss chickpeas with olive oil and ¼ teaspoon salt and pepper on a rimmed baking sheet. Roast for 30 to 40 minutes, tossing occasionally,until crisp.

3. Remove from the oven and stir with lemon zest in a mixing basin. Asthe chickpeas cool, they will crisp up even more.

Dressing And Salad:

1. Preheat the grill to medium heat. To make the dressing, purée all dressing ingredients in a small blender or food processor until smooth,adding 1 tablespoon water at a time to modify consistency and seasoning with salt and pepper to taste. Set aside the dressing.

2. To make the salad, follow these steps: 1 ½ tablespoons oil, brushed on the bread, 1 tablespoon oil, ¼ teaspoon salt, and ¼ teaspoon pepper, brushed on onion slices Season radishes with a pinch of salt and the remaining ½ tbsp oil. Using small skewers, thread radishes. 2 to 3 minutes per side on the grill, until toasted; immediately massage with garlic. Onions and radishes should be grilled until soft, about 5 minutesper side for onions and 6–8 minutes for radishes.

3. Separate the onion rings and tear the bread into pieces. Toss half of thedressing with the lettuce to coat it. Fold in the grilled croutons and onion rings gently. Serve with radish skewers, crispy chickpeas, and any leftover dressing for dipping or drizzling.

Nutrition:

Calories: 70 Carbohydrates: 5.8g Fiber: 1g Proteins: 2.9g

STEAK AND MUSHROOM NOODLES

Preparation time: 10 minutes

Cooking time: 12 minutes

Servings: 4

Ingredients:

- 100g shiitake mushrooms, halved, if large
- 100g chestnut mushrooms, sliced
- 150g udon noodles & 75g kale, finely chopped
- 75g baby leaf spinach, chopped
- 2 sirloin steaks & 2 teaspoons miso paste
- 2.5cm piece fresh ginger, finely chopped
- 1 star anise & 1 red chili, finely sliced
- 1 red onion, finely chopped
- 1 fresh coriander (cilantro) chopped
- 1 liter (1½ pints) warm water

Directions:

1. Spill the water into a saucepan and add in the miso, star anise, and ginger. Bring it to the boil, reduce the heat, and simmer gently. In themeantime, cook the noodles then drain them.

2. Warmth the oil in a saucepan, add the steak and cook for around 2-3minutes on each side. Remove the meat and set aside.

3. Place the mushrooms, spinach, coriander (cilantro), and kale into themiso broth and cook for 5 minutes.

4. Warmth the remaining oil in a separate pan and fry the chili and onionfor 4 minutes, until softened.

5. Serve the noodles into bowls and pour the soup on top.

6. Thinly slice the steaks and add them to the top. Serve immediately.

Nutrition:

Calories: 296 Carbohydrates: 24g Fat: 13g Proteins: 32

Masala Scallops

Preparation time: 10 minutes

Cooking time: 20 minutes

Servings: 4

Ingredients:

- 2 jalapenos, chopped
- 1 pound sea scallops
- A pinch of salt and black pepper
- ¼ teaspoon cinnamon powder
- 1 teaspoon garam masala
- 1 teaspoon coriander, ground
- 1 teaspoon cumin, ground
- 2 tablespoons cilantro

Directions:

1. Warmth up a pan with the oil over medium heat, add the jalapenos, cinnamon, and the other ingredients except for the scallops and cookfor 10 minutes.

Nutrition:

Calories: 251 Fat: 4g Carbohydrates: 11g Proteins: 17g

Lemongrass and Ginger Mackerel

Preparation time: 10 minutes

Cooking time: 25 minutes

Servings: 4

Ingredients:

- 4 mackerel filets, skinless and boneless
- 1 tablespoon ginger, grated
- 2 lemongrass sticks, chopped
- 2 red chilies, chopped
- Juice of 1 lime
- A handful parsley, chopped

Directions:

1. In a roasting pan, combine the mackerel with the oil, ginger, and theother ingredients, toss and bake at 390F for 25 minutes.

2. Divide everything between plates and serve.

Nutrition:

Calories: 251 Fat: 3g Carbohydrates: 14g Proteins: 8g

Snack

Smoky Red Pepper Hummus

Preparation time: 5 minutes

Cooking time: 0 minutes

Servings: 1 ½ cup

Ingredients:

- ¼ cup roasted red peppers
- 1 cup cooked chickpeas
- ⅛ teaspoon garlic powder
- ½ teaspoon salt
- ⅛ teaspoon ground black pepper
- ¼ teaspoon ground cumin
- ¼ teaspoon red chili powder
- 1 tablespoon Tahini
- 2 tablespoons water

Directions:

1. Set all the ingredients in the jar of the food processor and then pulseuntil smooth.

2. Tip the hummus in a bowl and then serve with vegetable slices.

Nutrition:

Calories: 489 Fat: 30g Proteins: 9g Carbohydrates: 15g Fiber: 6g

ROASTED TAMARI ALMONDS

Preparation time: 5 minutes

Cooking time: 10-15 minutes

Servings: 8

Ingredients:

- 1 pound (454 g) raw almonds
- 3 tablespoons tamari
- 1 tablespoon nutritional yeast
- 1 to 2 teaspoons chili powder

Directions:

1. Preheat the oven to 400F (205C). Set a large baking tray with parchment paper and set aside.

2. Mix the almonds and tamari in a medium bowl and toss to coat.

3. Arrange the almonds on the prepared baking tray in a single layer.

4. Roast in the preheated oven until browned, about 10 to 15 minutes. Setthe almonds halfway through the

5. Cooking time.

6. Let the almonds cool for 10 minutes in the baking tray. Sprinkle it with nutritional yeast and chili powder. Serve immediately, or store in the fridge for up to 2 weeks.

Nutrition:

Calories: 91 Fat: 28.3g Carbohydrates: 13.2g Proteins: 12.2g Fiber: 7.4g

TOMATILLO SALSA

Preparation time: 5 minutes

Cooking time: 15 minutes

Servings: 2 cups

Ingredients:

- 5 medium tomatillos, chopped
- 3 cloves of garlic, peeled, chopped
- 3 Roma tomatoes, chopped
- 1 jalapeno, chopped
- ½ of a red onion, peeled, chopped
- 1 Anaheim chili
- 2 teaspoons salt
- 1 teaspoon ground cumin
- 1 lime, juiced
- ¼ cup cilantro leaves
- ¾ cup of water

Directions:

1. Take a medium pot, place it over medium heat, pour in water, and then add onion, tomatoes, tomatillo, jalapeno, and Anaheim chili.

2. Sauté the vegetables for 15 minutes, remove the pot from heat, addcilantro and lime juice and then stir in salt.

3. Remove pot from heat and then pulse by using an immersion blenderuntil smooth.

4. Serve the salsa with chips.

Nutrition:

Calories: 317.4 Fat: 0g Proteins: 16g Carbohydrates: 64g Fiber: 16g

Arugula Pesto Couscous

Preparation time: 10 minutes

Cooking time: 16 minutes

Servings: 4

Ingredients:

- 8 ounces Israeli couscous
- 3 large tomatoes, chopped
- 3 cups arugula leaves
- ½ cup parsley leaves
- 6 cloves of garlic, peeled
- ½ cup walnuts
- ¾ teaspoon salt
- 1 cup and 1 tablespoon olive oil
- 2 cups vegetable broth

Directions:

1. Take a medium saucepan, place it over medium-high heat, add 1tablespoon of oil and then let it heat.

2. Add couscous, stir until mixed, and then cook for 4 minutes untilfragrant and toasted.

3. Pour in the broth, stir until mixed, bring it to a boil, switch heat to medium level and then simmer for 12 minutes until the couscous hasabsorbed all the liquid and turn tender.

4. When done, remove the pan from heat, fluff it with a fork, and then setaside until required.

5. While couscous cooks, prepare the pesto, and for this, place walnuts ina blender, add garlic, and then pulse until nuts have broken.

6. Add arugula, parsley, and salt, pulse until well combined, and thenblend in oil until smooth.

7. Transfer couscous to a salad bowl, add tomatoes and prepared

pesto,and then toss until mixed.

8. Serve straight away.

Nutrition:

Calories: 73 Fat: 4g Proteins: 2g Carbohydrates: 8g Fiber: 2g

Oatmeal and Raisin Balls

Preparation time: 40 minutes

Cooking time: 0 minutes

Servings: 12 balls

Ingredients:

- 1 cup rolled oats
- ¼ cup raisins
- ½ cup peanut butter

Directions:

1. Place oats in a large bowl, add raisins and peanut butter, and then stiruntil well combined.

2. Shape the mixture into twelve balls, 1 tablespoon of mixture per ball,and then arrange the balls on a baking sheet.

3. Bring the baking sheet into the freezer for 30 minutes until firm andthen serve.

Nutrition:

Calories: 135 Fat: 6g Proteins: 8g Carbohydrates: 13g Fiber: 4g

Oat Crunch Apple Crisp

Preparation time: 10 minutes

Cooking time: 35 minutes

Servings: 6

Ingredients:

- 3 medium apples, cored and cut into ¼ inch pieces
- ¾ cup apple juice
- 1 teaspoon vanilla extract
- 1 teaspoon ground cinnamon, divided
- 2 cups rolled oats
- ¼ cup maple syrup

Directions:

1. Warmth the oven to 375F

2. In a large bowl, merge the apple slices, apple juice, vanilla, and ½ teaspoon of cinnamon. Mix well to thoroughly coat the apple slices.

3. Layer the apple slices on the bottom of a round or square baking dish. Take any leftover liquid and pour it over the apple slices.

4. In a large bowl, stir together the oats, maple syrup, and the remaining ½ teaspoon of cinnamon until the oats are completely coated.

5. Sprinkle the oat mixture over the apples, being sure to spread it outevenly so that none of the apple slices are visible.

6. Bake for 35 minutes, or until the oats begin to turn golden brown, andserve.

Nutrition:

Calories: 150 Fat: 1.0g Carbohydrates: 25.9g Proteins: 17.1g Fiber: 2.0

PICO DE GALLO

Preparation time: 5 minutes

Cooking time: 0 minutes

Servings: 3

Ingredients:

- ½ of a medium red onion
- 2 cups diced tomato
- ½ cup chopped cilantro
- 1 jalapeno pepper, minced
- ⅛ teaspoon salt
- ¼ teaspoon ground black pepper
- ½ of a lime, juiced
- 1 teaspoon olive oil

Directions:

1. Take a large bowl, place all the ingredients in it and then stir until wellmixed.

2. Serve the Pico de Gallo with chips.

Nutrition:

Calories: 790 Fat: 6.4g Proteins: 25.6g Carbohydrates: 195.2g Fiber: 35.2g

Beet Balls

Preparation time: 10 minutes

Cooking time: 0 minutes

Servings: 18

Ingredients:

- ½ cup oats
- 1 medium beet, cooked
- ½ cup almond flour
- ⅓ cup shredded coconut and more for coating
- ¾ cup Medjool dates, pitted
- 1 tablespoon cocoa powder
- ½ cup peanuts
- ¼ cup chocolate chips, unsweetened

Directions:

1. Place cooked beets in a blender and then pulse until chopped into verysmall pieces.

2. Add remaining ingredients and then pulse until the dough comestogether.

3. Shape the dough into eighteen balls, coat them in some more coconutand then serve.

Nutrition:

Calories: 114.2 Fat: 2.4g Proteins: 5g Carbohydrates: 19.6g Fiber: 4.9g

CHEESY CRACKERS

Preparation time: 10 minutes

Cooking time: 15 to 20 minutes

Servings: 3

Ingredients:

- 1 ¾ cup almond meal & 3 tablespoons nutritional yeast
- ½ teaspoon of sea salt & 2 tablespoons lemon juice
- 1 tablespoon melted coconut oil
- 1 tablespoon ground flaxseed & 2 ½ tablespoons water

Directions:

1. Switch on the oven, then set it to 350 degrees F and let it preheat.

2. Meanwhile, take a medium bowl, place flaxseed in it, stir in water, and then let the mixture rest for 5 minutes until thickened.

3. Place almond meal in a medium bowl, add salt and yeast and then stiruntil mixed.

4. Add lemon juice and oil into the flaxseed mixture and then whisk untilmixed.

5. Pour the flaxseed mixture into the almond meal mixture and then stiruntil dough comes together.

6. Place a piece of wax paper on a clean working space, place the dough on it, secure with another piece of wax paper, and then roll dough into a ⅛-inch thick crust.

7. Cut the dough into a square shape, sprinkle salt over the top and thenbake for 15 to 20 minutes until done.

8. Serve straight away.

Nutrition:

Calories: 30 Fat: 1g Proteins: 1g Carbohydrates: 5g Fiber: 0g

CHOCOLATE PROTEIN BITES

Preparation time: 10 Minutes

Cooking time: 0 Minutes

Servings: 12

Ingredients:

- ½ cup Chocolate Protein Powder
- 1 Avocado, medium
- 1 tbsp. Chocolate Chips
- 1 tbsp. Almond Butter
- 1 tbsp. Cocoa Powder
- 1 tsp. Vanilla Extract
- Dash of Salt

Directions:

1. Begin by blending avocado, almond butter, vanilla extract, and salt in ahigh-speed blender until you get a smooth mixture.

2. Next, spoon in the protein powder, cocoa powder, and chocolate chipsto the blender.

3. Blend again until you get a smooth dough-like consistency mixture.

4. Now, check for seasoning and add more sweetness if needed.

5. Finally, with the help of a scooper, scoop out dough to make smallballs.

Nutrition:

Calories: 46 Proteins: 2g Carbohydrates: 2g Fat: 2g

Crunchy Granola

Preparation time: 10 Minutes

Cooking time: 20 Minutes

Servings: 1

Ingredients:

- ½ cup Oats
- Dash of Salt
- 2 tbsp. Vegetable Oil
- 3 tbsp. Maple Syrup
- ⅓ cup Apple Cider Vinegar
- ½ cup Almonds
- 1 tsp. Cardamom, grounded

Directions:

1. Preheat the oven to 375F.

2. After that, mix oats, pistachios, salt, and cardamom in a large bowl.

3. Next, spoon in the vegetable oil and maple syrup to the mixture.

4. Then, transfer the mixture to a parchment-paper-lined baking sheet.

5. Bake them for 13 minutes until the mixture is toasted. Tip: Check onthem now and then. Spread it out well.

6. Return the sheet to the oven for further ten minutes.

7. Detach the sheet from the oven and allow it to cool completely.

8. Serve and enjoy.

Nutrition:

Calories: 763 Proteins: 12.9g Carbohydrates: 64.8g Fat: 52.4g

Chocolate Almond Bars

Preparation time: 10 Minutes

Cooking time: 20 Minutes

Servings: 12

Ingredients:

- 1 cup Almonds
- 1 ½ cup Rolled Oats
- ⅓ cup Maple Syrup
- ¼ tsp. Sea Salt
- 5 oz. Protein Powder
- 1 tsp. Cinnamon

Directions:

1. For making these delicious vegan bars, you first need to place ¾ cup ofthe almonds and salt in the food processor.

2. Process them for a minute or until you get them in the form of almondbutter.

3. Now, swirl in the rest of the ingredients to the processor and processthem again until smooth.

4. Next, transfer the mixture to a greased parchment paper-lined bakingsheet and spread it across evenly.

5. Press them slightly down with the back of the spoon.

6. Chop down the remaining ¼ cup of the almonds and top it across themixture.

7. Finally, place them in the refrigerator for 20 minutes or until set.

Nutrition:

Calories: 166 Proteins: 12.8g Carbohydrates: 17.6g Fat: 6g

Spicy Nut and Seed Snack Mix

Preparation time: 5 Minutes

Cooking time: 5 Minutes

Servings: 4

Ingredients:

- ¼ tsp. garlic powder
- ¼ tsp. nutritional yeast
- ½ tsp. smoked paprika
- ¼ tsp. sea salt
- ¼ tsp. dried parsley
- ½ cup slivered almonds
- ½ cup cashew pieces
- ½ cup sunflower seeds
- ½ cup pepitas

Directions:

1. In a small bowl, merge the garlic powder, nutritional yeast, paprika,salt, and parsley. Set aside.

2. In a large skillet, add the almonds, cashews, sunflower seeds, pepitasand heat over low heat until warm and glistening, 3 minutes.

3. Set the heat off and stir in the parsley mixture.

4. Allow complete cooling and enjoy!

Nutrition:

Calories: 385 Proteins: 12g Carbohydrates: 16g Fat: 33g

FLAX CRACKERS

Preparation time: 5 Minutes

Cooking time: 1 hour 30 Minutes

Servings: 4 to 6

Ingredients:

- 1 cup Flax Seeds, whole
- 2 cups Water
- ¾ cup Flaxseeds, grounded
- 1 tsp. Sea Salt
- ½ cup Chia Seeds
- 1 tsp. Black Pepper
- ½ cup Sunflower Seeds

Directions:

1. First, place all the ingredients in a large mixing bowl and mix themwell. Soak them for 10 to 15 minutes.

2. After that, transfer the mixture to a parchment paper-lined baking sheetand spread it evenly. Tip: Make sure the paper lines the edges as well.

3. Next, bake it for 60 minutes at 350F.

4. Once the time is up, flip the entire bar and take off the parchmentpaper.

5. Bake for half an hour or until it becomes crispy and browned.

6. Allow it to cool completely and then break it down.

Nutrition:

Calories: 251 Proteins: 9.2g Carbohydrates: 14.9g Fat: 16g

Chocolate and Nuts Goji Bars

Preparation time: 5 Minutes

Cooking time: 0 Minutes

Servings: 4

Ingredients:

- 1 cup mixed nuts
- ¼ cup dried goji berries
- ¼ cup chopped pitted dates
- 2 tbsp. chocolate chips
- 1 ½ tsp. vanilla extract
- ¼ tsp. cinnamon powder
- 2 tbsp. vegetable oil
- 2 tbsp. golden flaxseed meal
- 1 tsp. maple syrup

Directions:

1. Attach all the ingredients to a blender and process until coarselysmooth.

2. Lay a large piece of plastic wrap on a flat surface and spread the batteron top. Bring another piece of plastic wrap on top and using a rolling pin, flatten the dough into a thick rectangle of about 1 ½ -inch thickness.

3. Remove the plastic wraps and use an oiled knife to cut the dough intobars.

4. Serve immediately and freeze any extras.

Nutrition:

Calories: 679 Proteins: 25g Carbohydrates: 11g Fat: 62g

CRANBERRY PROTEIN BARS

Preparation time: 5 Minutes

Cooking time: 2 hours

Servings: 4

Ingredients:

- 1½ cups cashew nut butter
- 3 scoops protein powder
- 4 tbsp. butter, melted
- 1 ½ tsp. maple syrup
- ½ tsp. salt or to taste
- 4 tbsp. dried cranberries, chopped

Directions:

1. Line a medium, shallow loaf pan with baking paper and set aside.

2. In a medium bowl, merge all the ingredients and spread in the loaf pan.Refrigerate for 2 hours until the batter is firm.

3. Remove the batter from the refrigerator and turn it onto a clean, flatsurface. Cut the batter into bars.

4. Serve, and freeze any extras.

Nutrition:

Calories: 968 Proteins: 29g Carbohydrates: 26g Fat: 86g

ONION RINGS

Preparation time: 15 minutes

Cooking time: 14 minutes

Servings: 4

Ingredients:

- 1 large sweet or Vidalia onion
- ½ cup chickpea flour
- ⅓ cup unsweetened plain plant-based milk
- 2 tablespoons freshly squeezed lemon juice
- 2 tablespoons No-Salt Hot Sauce
- 1 teaspoon No-Salt Spice Blend
- ⅔ cup panko breadcrumbs

Directions:

1. Peel off and discard the top ½ inch of the root end of the sweet onion. Continue cutting the onion into ½-inch-thick slices. Carefully separatethe slices into individual rings and set aside.

2. In a medium bowl, mix the chickpea flour, plant-based milk, lemon juice, hot sauce, and spice blend. Spill the breadcrumbs into a separatebowl.

3. Dip each ring into the chickpea batter so that it's completely and evenlycovered. Then dip the rings into the breadcrumbs and place them in the air fryer basket.

4. Fry at 380F for 14 minutes, or until the coating is browned and crispy.Be sure to flip your onion rings over halfway through cooking. Serve warm.

Nutrition:

Calories: 127 Fat: 2g Carbohydrates: 23g Fiber: 3g Proteins: 5g

FRENCH FRIES

Preparation time: 5 minutes

Cooking time: 15 minutes

Servings: 2

Ingredients:

- 1 large russet potato
- ¼ cup freshly squeezed lemon juice
- 3 tablespoons nutritional yeast
- 1 tablespoon No-Salt Spice Blend

Directions:

1. Cut the potato lengthwise into ½-inch-thick fries.

2. Pour the lemon juice onto a plate. On a second plate, mix the nutritionalyeast and spice blend. Dip the fries, one at a time, into the lemon juice. Shake off the excess juice and dip the fries into the spice mixture to completely cover them on all sides. Once covered, place the fries in a single layer in the air fryer basket or on the rack.

3. Fry at 400F for 15 minutes until the fries are crispy. Shake up thebasket or turn the fries over halfway through cooking. Serve immediately.

Nutrition:

Calories: 172 Fat: 0g Carbohydrates: 36g Fiber: 3g Proteins: 6g

Roasted Asparagus

Preparation time: 10 minutes

Cooking time: 5 minutes

Servings: 4

Ingredients:

- 1 tablespoon tahini
- 1 tablespoon freshly squeezed lemon juice
- 1 tablespoon water
- 1 teaspoon No-Salt Spice Blend
- 1 pound fresh asparagus, woody ends trimmed

Directions:

1. In a large bowl, merge together the tahini, lemon juice, water, and spiceblend until well combined.

2. Attach the asparagus to the bowl and toss to coat.

3. Place the coated spears in a single layer in the air fryer basket or on therack and roast at 400F for 5 minutes, or until the tips start to brown andthe insides are cooked but not mushy. Serve warm.

Nutrition:

Calories: 46 Fat: 2g Carbohydrates: 5g Fiber: 3g Proteins: 3g

Twice-Baked Potatoes

Preparation time: 15 minutes

Cooking time: 35 minutes

Servings: 4

Ingredients:

- 2 medium russet potatoes, halved lengthwise
- ½ cup No-Cheese Sauce
- 2 scallions
- 1 tablespoon nutritional yeast

Directions:

1. Place each potato, cut-side down, on a scrap of parchment paper in theair fryer basket or on the rack. Roast at 400F for 30 minutes.

2. Carefully detach the potatoes from the air fryer. Set out the middle ofeach potato, leaving ¼ inch of flesh around the edges, and place the scooped parts in a medium bowl. Add the no-cheese sauce, scallions,and nutritional yeast to the bowl and mix until well combined.

3. Equally spoon the mixture into the potato skins and place them back inthe air fryer. Grill at 400F for 3 to 4 minutes, or until the tops get crispy. Serve warm.

Nutrition:

Calories: 178 Fat: 21g Carbohydrates: 37g Fiber: 3g Proteins: 7g

BABA GHANOUSH

Preparation time: 10 minutes

Cooking time: 30 minutes

Servings: 2

Ingredients:

- 1 medium eggplant
- 2 tablespoons tahini
- 2 tablespoons freshly squeezed lemon juice
- 1 teaspoon granulated garlic
- ¼ teaspoon ground cumin
- Freshly chopped parsley, for garnish

Directions:

1. Place the whole eggplant in a pan in the air fryer. Roast at 400°F for 30 minutes, carefully turning the eggplant over halfway through cooking.

2. Let the eggplant cool for 5 to 10 minutes. Then set out the flesh and setit in a medium bowl. Drain as much water from the eggplant flesh as possible.

3. Add the tahini, lemon juice, granulated garlic, and cumin to the bowl.Mix until well combined. Garnish with the parsley.

Nutrition:

Calories: 169 Fat: 9g Carbohydrates: 22g Fiber: 10g Proteins: 6g

Citrus-Roasted Brussels sprouts

Preparation time: 10 minutes

Cooking time: 10 minutes

Servings: 4

Ingredients:

- ¼ cup freshly squeezed orange juice
- 1 teaspoon pure maple syrup
- 1 tablespoon balsamic vinegar
- 1 pound Brussels sprouts, trimmed and quartered

Directions:

1. In a large bowl, set together the orange juice, maple syrup, and balsamic vinegar. Add the Brussels sprouts to the bowl and toss untilwell coated.

2. Place the Brussels sprouts, cut-side up, in a single layer in the air fryerbasket or on the rack. Roast at 400F until they start to crisp up. Be careful not to burn them!

Nutrition:

Calories: 64 Fat: 0g Carbohydrates: 14g Fiber: 4g Proteins: 4g

BERRY AND YOGURT SMOOTHIE

Preparation time: 5 minutes

Cooking time: 0 minutes.

Servings: 2

Ingredients:

- 2 small bananas
- 3 cups frozen mixed berries
- 1(½) cup cashew yogurt
- ½ teaspoon vanilla extract, unsweetened
- ½ cup almond milk, unsweetened

Directions:

1. Place all the ingredients in the order to a food processor or blender andthen pulse for 2 to 3 minutes at high speed until smooth.

2. Pour the smoothie into two glasses and then serve.

Nutrition:

Calories: 326 Fat: 6.5g Carbohydrates: 65.6g Proteins: 8g Fiber: 8.4g

Basil Lime Green Tea

Preparation time: 5 minutes

Cooking time: 4 minutes

Servings: 8

Ingredients:

- 8 cups of filtered water
- 10 bags of green tea
- ¼ tsp. of maple syrup
- A pinch of baking soda
- Lime slices to taste
- Lemon slices to taste
- Basil leaves to taste

Directions:

1. Add water, maple syrup, and baking soda to the pot and mix. Add thetea bags and cover. Cook on High for 4 minutes. Open and serve withlime slices, lemon slices, and basil leaves.

Nutrition:

Calories: 32 Carbohydrates: 8g Fat: 0g Proteins: 0g

PINEAPPLE AND SPINACH JUICE

Preparation time: 5 minutes

Cooking time: 0 minutes

Servings: 2

Ingredients:

- 2 medium red apples, cored, peeled, chopped
- 3 cups spinach
- ½ of a medium pineapple, peeled
- 2 lemons, peeled

Directions:

1. Process all the ingredients in the order in a juicer or blender and thenstrain it into two glasses.

2. Serve straight away.

Nutrition:

Calories: 131 Fat: 0.5g Carbohydrates: 34.5g Proteins: 1.7g Fiber: 5g

Strawberry and Chocolate Milkshake

Preparation time: 5 minutes

Cooking time: 0 minutes

Servings: 2

Ingredients:

- 2 cups frozen strawberries
- 3 tablespoons cocoa powder
- 1 scoop protein powder
- 2 tablespoons maple syrup
- 1 teaspoon vanilla extract, unsweetened
- 2 cups almond milk, unsweetened

Directions:

1. Place all the ingredients in the order to a food processor or blender andthen pulse for 2 to 3 minutes at high speed until smooth.

2. Pour the smoothie into two glasses and then serve.

Nutrition:

Calories: 199 Fat: 4.1g Carbohydrates: 40.5g Proteins: 3.7g Fiber: 5.5g

Fruit Infused Water

Preparation time: 5 minutes

Cooking time: 0 minutes

Servings: 2

Ingredients:

- 3 strawberries, sliced
- 5 mint leaves
- ½ of orange, sliced
- 2 cups of water

Directions:

1. Divide fruits and mint between two glasses, pour in water, stir until justmixed, and refrigerate for 2 hours.

2. Serve straight away.

Nutrition:

Calories: 5.4 Fat: 0.1g Carbohydrates: 1.3g Proteins: 0.1g Fiber: 0.4g

LEBANESE POTATO SALAD

Preparation time: 5 minutes

Cooking time: 10 minutes

Servings: 4

Ingredients:

- 1-pound Russet potatoes
- 1(½) tablespoon extra-virgin olive oil
- 2 scallions, thinly sliced
- Freshly ground pepper to taste
- 2 tablespoons lemon juice
- ¼ tsp. salt or to taste
- 2 tablespoons fresh mint leaves, chopped

Directions:

1. Set a saucepan half-filled with water over medium heat. Add salt and potatoes and cook for 10 minutes until tender. Drain the potatoes and set them in a bowl of cold water. When cool enough to handle, peel andcube the potatoes. Place in a bowl.

2. To make the dressing: Add oil, lemon juice, salt, and pepper in a bowland whisk well. Drizzle dressing over the potatoes. Toss well.

3. Add scallions and mint and toss well.

4. Divide into 4 plates and serve.

Nutrition:

Calories: 129 Fat: 0.9g Carbohydrates: 8.8g

Kale and Cauliflower Salad

Preparation time: 10 minutes

Cooking time: 0 minutes

Servings: 2

Ingredients:

- ½ cup lemon juice
- 1 tablespoon olive oil
- 1 teaspoon maple syrup
- ⅛ teaspoon salt
- ¼ teaspoon ground black pepper
- 1 bunch kale, cut into bite-size pieces
- ½ cup roasted cauliflower
- ½ cup dried cranberries

Directions:

1. Whisk lemon juice, olive oil, maple syrup, salt, and black pepper in alarge bowl. Add kale, cauliflower, and cranberries; toss to combine.

Nutrition:

Calories: 76 Fat: 5 g Carbohydrates: 5.9 g

Dessert

Berries Pie

Preparation time: 10 minutes

Cooking time: 24 minutes

Servings: 12

Ingredients:

- 2 cups coconut flour
- 1 cup coconut butter, soft
- 1 cup pecans, chopped
- 1 and ¼ cup coconut sugar
- 4 cups rhubarb, chopped
- 1 cup strawberries, sliced
- 8 ounces coconut cream

Directions:

1. In a bowl, merge the flour with the butter, pecans and ¼ cup of sugarand mix well.

2. Transfer this to a cake pan, press firmly into the pan, place in the ovenand bake at 350F for 20 minutes.

3. In a pan combine the strawberries with the remaining ingredients, mixwell and cook over medium heat for 4 minutes.

4. Spread it on the crust of the cake and keep it in the fridge for a fewhours before slicing and serving.

Nutrition:

Calories: 332 Fat: 5g Fiber: 5g Carbohydrates: 15g Proteins: 6.3g

Vanilla and Apple Brownies

Preparation time: 10 minutes

Cooking time: 20 minutes

Servings: 12

Ingredients:

- 1 and ½ cups apples, cored and cubed
- 2 tablespoons stevia
- ½ cup quick oats
- 2 tablespoons cocoa powder
- ⅓ cup coconut cream
- ¼ cup coconut oil, melted
- ½ teaspoon baking powder
- 2 teaspoons vanilla extract
- Cooking spray

Directions:

1. In your food processor, combine the apples with the stevia and theother ingredients except for the cooking spray and blend well.

2. Grease a square pan with cooking spray, add the apples mix, spread, introduce in the oven, and bake at 350F for 20 minutes, leave aside tocool down, slice, and serve.

Nutrition:

Calories: 200 Fat: 3g Fiber: 3g Carbohydrates: 14g Proteins: 4g

Banana Cake

Preparation time: 10 minutes

Cooking time: 25 minutes

Servings: 8

Ingredients:

- 2 cups almond flour
- ¼ cup cocoa powder
- 1 banana, peeled and mashed
- ½ teaspoon baking soda
- ½ cup coconut sugar
- ¾ cup almond milk
- ¼ cup coconut oil, melted
- 2 tablespoons flaxseed mixed with 3 tablespoons water
- 1 teaspoon vanilla extract
- 1 tablespoon lemon juice
- Cooking spray

Directions:

1. In a bowl, merge the flour with the cocoa powder, banana, and theother ingredients except for the cooking spray and stir well.

2. Grease a cake pan with cooking spray, pour the cake mix, spread, bakein the oven at 350F for 25 minutes, cool down, slice, and serve.

Nutrition:

Calories: 245 Fat: 5.6g Fiber: 4g Carbohydrates: 17g Proteins: 4g

COCONUT MOUSSE

Preparation time: 10 minutes

Cooking time: 0 minutes

Servings: 12

Ingredients:

- 2 and ¾ cup almond milk
- 2 tablespoons cocoa powder
- 1 teaspoon coconut extract
- 1 teaspoon vanilla extract
- 4 teaspoons stevia
- 1 cup coconut, toasted

Directions:

1. In a bowl, merge the almond milk with cocoa powder and the otheringredients, whisk well, divide into small cups and serve cold.

Nutrition:

Calories: 352 Fat: 5.4g Fiber: 5.4g Carbohydrates: 11g Proteins: 3g

Mango Coconut Pudding

Preparation time: 10 minutes

Cooking time: 50 minutes

Servings: 4

Ingredients:

- 1 cup coconut, shredded
- 1 cup coconut cream
- 1 mango, peeled and chopped
- 1 cup coconut milk
- 2 tablespoons coconut sugar
- 1 teaspoon vanilla extract
- ½ teaspoon cinnamon powder

Directions:

1. In a pan, mix the coconut with the cream and the other ingredients, stir, simmer for 50 minutes over medium heat, divide into bowls and serve cold.

Nutrition:

Calories: 251 Fat: 3.6g Fiber: 4g Carbohydrates: 16g Proteins: 7.1g

RHUBARB AND BERRIES PIE

Preparation time: 10 minutes

Cooking time: 25 minutes

Servings: 12

Ingredients:

- 2 cups coconut flour
- 1 cup coconut butter, soft
- 1 cup pecans, chopped
- 1 and ¼ cup coconut sugar
- 4 cups rhubarb, chopped
- 1 cup strawberries, sliced
- 8 ounces coconut cream

Directions:

1. In a bowl, merge the flour with the butter, pecans, and ¼ cup sugar andstir well.

2. Transfer this to a pie pan, press well into the pan, introduce it in theoven and bake at 350F for 20 minutes.

3. In a pan, combine the strawberries with the remaining ingredients, stirwell and cook over medium heat for 4 minutes.

4. Spread this over the pie crust and keep it in the fridge for a few hoursbefore slicing and serving.

Nutrition:

Calories: 332 Fat: 6g Fiber: 5g Carbohydrates: 15g Proteins: 6.3g

BANANA SALAD

Preparation time: 10 minutes

Cooking time: 0 minutes

Servings: 2

Ingredients:

- ¼ cantaloupe, cubed
- 3 bananas, cut into chunks
- 1 apple, cored and cut into chunks
- 1 tablespoon stevia
- 1 teaspoon vanilla extract
- Juice of 1 lime

Directions:

1. In a bowl, merge the cantaloupe with the bananas and the other ingredients, toss and serve.

Nutrition:

Calories: 126 Fat: 3.3g Fiber: 1g Carbohydrates: 1.2g Proteins: 2g

Lemon Berries

Preparation time: 10 minutes

Cooking time: 10 minutes

Servings: 6

Ingredients:

- 2 teaspoons lemon juice
- 2 teaspoons lemon zest, grated
- Juice of 1 apple
- 1 teaspoon vanilla extract
- 1 pound blackberries
- 1 pound strawberries
- 4 tablespoons stevia

Directions:

1. In a pan, mix the berries with the stevia and the other ingredients, stirand cook over medium heat for 10 minutes.

2. Divide into cups and serve cold.

Nutrition:

Calories: 170 Fat: 3.4g Fiber: 3g Carbohydrates: 4g Proteins: 4g

PEACH STEW

Preparation time: 10 minutes

Cooking time: 10 minutes

Servings: 6

Ingredients:

- 1 pound peaches, peeled and chopped
- 2 tablespoons water
- 2 tablespoons stevia
- 2 tablespoons lemon juice
- ¼ teaspoon almond extract

Directions:

1. In a pot, combine the peaches with the water and the other ingredients, toss well, cook over medium heat for 10 minutes, divide into bowls andserve.

Nutrition:

Calories: 160 Fat: 3.8g Fiber: 2g Carbohydrates: 6g Proteins: 6g

APPLE STEW

Preparation time: 10 minutes

Cooking time: 15 minutes

Servings: 6

Ingredients:

- 6 apples, cored and roughly chopped
- 4 tablespoons stevia
- 2 teaspoons vanilla extract
- 2 teaspoons lime juice
- 2 teaspoons cinnamon powder

Directions:

1. In a small pan, combine the apples with the stevia and the other ingredients, heat up and cook for about 10-15 minutes, divide betweensmall dessert plates and serve.

Nutrition:

Calories: 210 Fat: 7.3g Fiber: 3g Carbohydrates: 8g Proteins: 5g

MINTY APRICOTS

Preparation time: 10 minutes

Cooking time: 10 minutes

Servings: 4

Ingredients:

- ⅓ cup water
- 2 pounds apricots, chopped
- 3 tablespoons stevia
- 1 tablespoon mint, chopped

Directions:

1. In a pot, mix the apricots with the stevia and the other ingredients, stir,cook for 10 minutes, divide into bowls and serve.

Nutrition:

Calories: 160 Fat: 5.1g Fiber: 4g Carbohydrates: 8g Proteins: 5.2g

MANGO MIX

Preparation time: 10 minutes

Cooking time: 10 minutes

Servings: 8

Ingredients:

- 1 and ½ pounds mango, peeled and cubed
- 3 tablespoons stevia
- 1 cup orange juice
- ½ tablespoon lime juice
- 1 teaspoon vanilla extract

Directions:

1. In a small pot, combine the mango with the stevia, orange juice, and theother ingredients, toss, bring to a parboil over medium heat, cook for 10minutes, divide into bowls and serve.

Nutrition:

Calories: 160 Fat: 5.4g Fiber: 4g Carbohydrates: 8g Proteins: 3.4g

BLUEBERRY STEW

Preparation time: 10 minutes

Cooking time: 10 minutes

Servings: 4

Ingredients:

- 2 tablespoons lemon juice
- 3 tablespoons stevia
- 12 ounces blueberries
- 1 cup orange juice
- 1 teaspoon vanilla extract

Directions:

1. In a pot, mix the blueberries with the stevia and the other ingredients, stir, cook over medium heat for 10 minutes, divide into small cups andserve cold.

Nutrition:

Calories: 201 Fat: 3g Fiber: 2g Carbohydrates: 6g Proteins: 3.8g

LIME CREAM

Preparation time: 10 minutes

Cooking time: 15 minutes

Servings: 4

Ingredients:

- 3 cups coconut milk
- Juice of 2 limes
- Lemon zest of 2 limes, grated
- 3 tablespoons stevia
- 3 tablespoons coconut oil
- 2 tablespoons gelatin
- 1 cup water

Directions:

1. In your blender, mix coconut milk with lime juice and the otheringredients except for the water and blend well.

2. Divide this into small jars and seal them.

3. Put the jars in a pan, add the water, introduce in the oven and cook at380 degrees F for 15 minutes.

4. Serve the cream cold.

Nutrition:

Calories: 161 Fat: 3.4g Fiber: 5g Carbohydrates: 6g Proteins: 4g

Vanilla Peach Mix

Preparation time: 10 minutes

Cooking time: 10 minutes

Servings: 4

Ingredients:

- 4 cups water
- 3 peaches, chopped
- 2 cups rolled oats
- 1 teaspoon vanilla extract
- 2 tablespoons flax meal

Directions:

1. In a pan, combine the peaches with the water and the other ingredients,stir, bring to a parboil over medium heat, cook for 10 minutes, divide into bowls and serve.

Nutrition:

Calories: 161 Fat: 3g Fiber: 3g Carbohydrates: 7g Proteins: 5g

PEAR STEW

Preparation time: 10 minutes

Cooking time: 10 minutes

Servings: 4

Ingredients:

- 3 pears, cored and chopped
- 2 tablespoons stevia
- ¼ cup coconut, shredded
- ½ teaspoon cinnamon powder
- 3 tablespoons coconut oil, melted
- ¼ cup pecans, chopped

Directions:

1. In a pan, combine pears with the stevia and the other ingredients, stir,cook for 8 minutes, divide into bowls and serve cold.

Nutrition:

Calories: 142 Fat: 4g Fiber: 4g Carbohydrates: 7.2g Proteins: 7g

MANGO SHAKE

Preparation time: 5 minutes

Cooking time: 0 minutes

Servings: 2

Ingredients:

- 2 medium mangoes, peeled
- 2 teaspoons cocoa powder
- ½ big avocado, mashed
- ¾ cup almond milk
- 1 tablespoon stevia

Directions:

1. In a blender, mix the mangoes with the cocoa powder and the otheringredients, blend, divide into glasses and serve.

Nutrition:

Calories: 185 Fat: 3.4g Fiber: 4.2g Carbohydrates: 6g Proteins: 7g

Lime Bars

Preparation time: 30 minutes

Cooking time: 0 minutes

Servings: 4

Ingredients:

- 1 cup avocado oil
- 2 bananas, peeled and chopped
- A pinch of salt
- 3 tablespoons stevia
- ¼ cup lime juice
- A pinch of lime zest, grated
- Cooking spray
- 3 kiwis, peeled and chopped

Directions:

1. In a food processor, mix the oil with the bananas and the other ingredients except for the cooking spray pulse and spread it into a panafter you've greased it with the cooking spray.

2. Keep in the fridge for 30 minutes, slice, and serve bars.

Nutrition:

Calories: 187 Fat: 3g Fiber: 3g Carbohydrates: 4g Proteins: 4g

BLACKBERRY COBBLER

Preparation time: 10 minutes

Cooking time: 30 minutes

Servings: 6

Ingredients:

- ¾ cup coconut sugar
- 6 cups blackberries
- ⅛ teaspoon baking soda
- 1 tablespoon lemon juice
- ½ cup almond flour
- A pinch of salt
- ½ cup water
- 3 and ½ tablespoon avocado oil
- Cooking spray

Directions:

1. Set a baking dish with some cooking spray and leave it aside.

2. In a bowl, mix blackberries with half of the coconut sugar, sprinkle some flour and add lemon juice, whisk and pour into the baking dish.

3. In another bowl, mix flour with remaining sugar, a pinch of salt, bakingsoda, ½ cup water, and the oil and stir well with your hands.

4. Spread over berries, bake at 375 degrees F for 30 minutes, cool down,and serve.

Nutrition:

Calories: 221 Fat: 7.3g Fiber: 3.3g Carbohydrates: 6g Proteins: 9g

BLACK TEA CAKE

Preparation time: 10 minutes

Cooking time: 35 minutes

Servings: 12

Ingredients:

- 6 tablespoons black tea powder
- 2 cups almond milk
- ½ cup coconut butter
- 2 cups coconut sugar
- 2 tablespoons flaxseed mixed with 3 tablespoons water
- 2 teaspoons vanilla extract
- ½ cup olive oil
- 3 and ½ cups almond flour
- 1 teaspoon baking soda
- 3 teaspoons baking powder

Directions:

1. In a large bowl, mix the black tea powder with the almond milk,coconut butter, and the other ingredients and stir well.

2. Pour this into a lined cake pan, place in the oven at 350 degrees F andbake for 30 minutes. Leave cakes to cool down.

3. Slice and serve.

Nutrition:

Calories: 200 Fat: 6.5g Fiber: 4g Carbohydrates: 6.5g Proteins: 4.5g

Green Tea Avocado Pudding

Preparation time: 2 hours

Cooking time: 5 minutes

Servings: 6

Ingredients:

- 2 cups almond milk
- 2 tablespoons green tea powder
- 1 cup coconut cream
- 3 tablespoons stevia
- 1 avocado, peeled, pitted, and mashed
- 1 teaspoon gelatin powder

Directions:

1. In a pan, mix the almond milk with green tea powder and the other ingredients, stir, cook for 5 minutes, divide into cups and keep in thefridge for 2 hours before serving.

Nutrition:

Calories: 210 Fat: 4.4g Fiber: 3g Carbohydrates: 7g Proteins: 4g

Pineapple and Mango Oatmeal

Preparation time: 5 minutes

Cooking time: 0 minutes

Servings: 2

Ingredients:

- 2 cups unsweetened almond milk
- 2 cups rolled oats
- ½ cup pineapple chunks, thawed if frozen
- ½ cup diced mango, thawed if frozen
- 1 banana, sliced
- 1 tablespoon chia seeds
- 1 tablespoon maple syrup

Directions:

1. Stir together the almond milk, oats, pineapple, mango, banana, chiaseeds, and maple syrup in a large bowl until you see no clumps.

2. Secure and refrigerate to chill for at least 4 hours, preferably overnight.

3. Serve chilled with your favorite toppings.

Nutrition:

Calories: 512 Fat: 22.1g Carbohydrates: 13.1g Proteins: 14.1g Fiber: 15.2g

Breakfast Quinoa

Preparation time: 5 minutes

Cooking time: 10 minutes

Servings: 2

Ingredients:

- 1 cup unsweetened almond milk
- 2 cups cooked quinoa
- 1 tablespoon defatted peanut powder
- 1 tablespoon cocoa powder
- 1 tablespoon maple syrup

Directions:

1. Add the almond milk to a saucepan over medium-high heat and bringto a boil.

2. Set the heat to low, and add the quinoa, peanut powder, cocoa powder,and maple syrup while whisking.

3. Allow to simmer for 6 minutes, stirring frequently, or until some liquidhas evaporated.

4. Remove from the heat and serve warm.

Nutrition:

Calories: 340 Fat: 18.2g Carbohydrates: 3.1g Proteins: 14.2g Fiber: 7.1g

Strawberry Chia Jam

Preparation time: 10 minutes

Cooking time: 20 minutes

Servings: 2

Ingredients:

- 1 pound (454 g) fresh strawberries, hulled and halved
- ¼ cup maple syrup
- ¼ cup water
- 3 tbsp. freshly squeezed lemon juice (from 1 lemon)
- 3 tablespoons chia seeds
- 1 teaspoon vanilla extract

Directions:

1. Add the strawberries, maple syrup, water, and lemon juice to a mediumsaucepan over medium heat. Allow to parboil for about 15 minutes, stirring occasionally, or until the strawberries begin to soften and bubble. Mash the strawberries to your desired consistency.

2. Add the chia seeds and continue stirring over low heat for 5 minutes.The chia seeds will help the jam achieve a gelatinous texture.

3. Add the vanilla and stir until combined. Detach from the heat and letthe jam cool to room temperature. Stir again.

4. Serve immediately.

Nutrition:

Calories: 132 Fat: 2.5g Carbohydrates: 25.7g Proteins: 1.9g Fiber: 2.5g

STICKY RICE CONGEE WITH DATES

Preparation time: 10 minutes

Cooking time: 15 minutes

Servings: 4

Ingredients:

- 2 cups water
- 4 cups cooked brown rice
- ½ cup chopped apricots
- ½ cup dates, pitted and chopped
- ¼ teaspoon ground cloves
- 1 large cinnamon stick
- Salt, to taste (optional)

Directions:

1. Add 2 cups of water to a large saucepan over medium heat and bring toa boil.

2. Add the brown rice, apricots, dates, cloves, and cinnamon stick, and stirwell.

3. Set the heat to medium-low and parboil for 15 minutes, stirring occasionally, or until the mixture is thickened. Sprinkle the salt toseason, if desired.

4. Let the congee cool for 5 minutes and remove the cinnamon stick, thenserve.

Nutrition:

Calories: 313 Fat: 1.9g Carbohydrates: 68.8g Proteins: 6.0g Fiber: 6.2g

Easy Apple and Cinnamon Muesli

Preparation time: 10 minutes

Cooking time: 0 minutes

Servings: 2

Ingredients:

- 1 cup rolled oats
- ½ cup raisins
- ¾ cup unsweetened almond milk
- 2 tablespoons date molasses (optional)
- ¼ teaspoon ground cinnamon
- 1 Granny Smith apple, grated

Directions:

1. In a large bowl, merge the oats, raisins, almond milk, date molasses (ifdesired), and cinnamon. Stir until well combined and transfer the bowlto the fridge. Let the oats soak for at least 30 minutes.

2. Remove from the fridge and add the grated apple. Give it a good stirand serve immediately.

Nutrition:

Calories: 325 Fat: 4.2g Carbohydrates: 63.7g Proteins: 8.8g Fiber: 10.1g

SALTED CARAMEL OATMEAL

Preparation time: 5 minutes

Cooking time: 15 minutes

Servings: 4

Ingredients:

- 4 cups water
- 16 Medjool dates, pitted and chopped
- Pinch salt (optional)
- 2 cups steel-cut oats
- Fresh berries, for topping (optional)
- Sliced almonds, for topping (optional)

Directions:

1. Put the water, dates, and salt (if desired) in a small saucepan over highheat and bring to a rapid boil.

2. Once it starts to boil. Add the oats and allow to simmer for 10 minutes,stirring frequently, or until the oats are cooked through.

3. Divide the oatmeal among four serving bowls. Serve topped with freshberries and sliced almonds, if desired.

Nutrition:

Calories: 376 Fat: 2.1g Carbohydrates: 84.9g Proteins: 5.2g Fiber: 9.1g

CREAMY BROWN RICE CEREAL WITH RAISINS

Preparation time: 5 minutes

Cooking time: 10 minutes

Servings: 2

Ingredients:

- 2 cups water
- ½ cup uncooked brown rice
- ¼ cup raisins
- 1½ cups unsweetened almond milk (optional)
- ½ teaspoon cinnamon (optional)

Directions:

1. Add the water to a medium saucepan over medium-high heat and bringto a boil.

2. Meanwhile, pulverize the brown rice by using a high-speed blender or food processor. Grind until the rice resembles sand.

3. Once it starts to boil, gradually stir in the ground brown rice.

4. Add the raisins and set the heat to low. Secure and simmer for 5 to 8minutes, stirring once or twice during cooking, or until the rice is tender.

5. Sprinkle with the almond milk and cinnamon, if desired.

Nutrition:

Calories: 131 Fat: 1.8g Carbohydrates: 26.5g Proteins: 2.4g Fiber: 1.3g

CASHEW-DATE WAFFLES

Preparation time: 20 minutes

Cooking time: 10 minutes

Servings: 2

Ingredients:

- 1 ounce (28 g) raw, unsalted cashews (about ¼ cup)
- 1 ounce (28 g) pitted dates, chopped
- 2 cups unsweetened coconut milk
- 1½ cups old-fashioned rolled oats
- ½ cup cornmeal & 2 teaspoons baking powder
- ½ teaspoon cinnamon

Directions:

1. In a small bowl, add the cashews, dates, and coconut milk. Let the nutsand dates soak in the milk for at least 15 minutes.

2. Merge the rolled oats in a blender until it has reached a powderyconsistency.

3. Place the oats in a medium bowl, along with the cornmeal, bakingpowder, and cinnamon. Stir well and set aside.

4. Preheat the waffle iron to medium-high heat.

5. Blend the cashews, dates, and coconut milk in a blender until completely mixed. Spill the mixture into the bowl of dry ingredientsand whisk to combine. Let the batter sit for 1 minute.

6. Slowly pour ½ to ¾ cup of the batter into the preheated waffle iron andcook until golden brown. Repeat with the remaining batter.

7. Divide the waffles between two plates and serve warm.

Nutrition:

Calories: 849 Fat: 13.5g Carbohydrates: 66.4g Proteins: 16.8g Fiber: 10.1g

Maple Sunflower Seed Granola

Preparation time: 20 minutes

Cooking time: 0 minutes

Servings: 2

Ingredients:

- 1½ cups peanut butter
- ¼ cup maple syrup
- 1½ cups old-fashioned rolled oats
- ¾ cup raw sunflower seeds
- ¾ cup flaxseed meal

Directions:

1. Set the peanut butter and maple syrup in a microwave-safe bowl, and microwave on high, stirring well between each interval, until the mixture is completely mixed. Let it rest for a few minutes until slightlycooled.

2. Add the rolled oats, sunflower seeds, and flaxseed meal to the bowl,and whisk until well incorporated.

3. Set the mixture to a baking sheet lined with parchment paper andspread it out into an even layer.

4. Transfer the baking sheet in the freezer for at least 25 minutes untilfirm.

5. Remove from the freezer and break the granola into large chunksbefore serving.

Nutrition:

Calories: 764 Fat: 51.7g Carbohydrates: 47.8g Proteins: 27.0g Fiber: 16.0g

Vegan Dairy Free Breakfast Bowl

Preparation time: 20 minutes

Cooking time: 0 minutes

Servings: 2

Ingredients:

- ½ cup strawberries
- ½ cup blueberries
- ½ cup blackberries
- ½ cup raspberries
- 1 grapefruit, peeled and segmented
- 3 tbs. fresh orange juice (from 1 orange)
- 1 tablespoon pure maple syrup
- ¼ cup chopped fresh mint
- ¼ cup sliced almonds

Directions:

1. In a serving bowl, combine the berries and grapefruit.

2. In a bowl, stir together the orange juice and maple syrup.

3. Pour the syrup mixture over the fruit. Sprinkle it with the mint andalmonds. Serve immediately

Nutrition:

Calories: 199 Fat: 4g Fiber: 3g Carbohydrates: 12g Proteins: 9g

HOT AND HEALTHY BREAKFAST BOWL WITH NUTS

Preparation time: 5 minutes

Cooking time: 0 minutes

Servings: 1

Ingredients:

- ½ cup oats, or quinoa flakes
- 1 tablespoon ground flaxseed, or chia seeds, or hemp hearts
- 1 tablespoon maple syrup or coconut sugar (optional)
- ¼ teaspoon ground cinnamon (optional)
- 1 apple, chopped and 1 tablespoon walnuts
- 2 tablespoons dried cranberries and 1 tablespoon pumpkin seeds
- 1 pear, chopped and 1 tablespoon cashews
- 1 cup sliced grapes and 1 tablespoon sunflower seeds
- 1 banana, sliced, and 1 tablespoon peanut butter
- 2 tablespoons raisins and 1 tablespoon hazelnuts
- 1 cup berries and 1 tablespoon unsweetened coconut flakes

Directions:

1. Mix the oats, flax, maple syrup, and cinnamon (if using) together in abowl or to-go container (a travel mug or short thermos works beautifully).

2. Pour enough cool water over the oats to submerge them and stir to combine. Leave to soak for a minimum of half an hour, or overnight.

3. Add your choice of toppings.

4. Boil about ½ cup water and pour over the oats. Let them soak for about5 minutes before eating.

Nutrition:

Calories: 244 Fat: 16g Carbohydrates: 10g Fiber: 6g Proteins: 7g

HEALTHY CHOCOLATE OATS BITES

Preparation time: 15 minutes

Cooking time: 12 minutes

Servings: 2

Ingredients:

- 1 tablespoon ground flaxseed
- 2 tbsp. almond butter or sunflower seed butter
- 2 tablespoons maple syrup
- 1 banana, mashed
- 1 teaspoon ground cinnamon
- ¼ teaspoon ground nutmeg (optional)
- Pinch sea salt
- ½ cup rolled oats
- ¼ cup raisins, or dark chocolate chips

Directions:

1. Preheat the oven to 350F. Set a large baking sheet with parchment paper. Merge the ground flax with just enough water to cover it in asmall dish and leave it to sit.

2. In a large bowl, merge together the almond butter and maple syrup untilcreamy, then attach the banana. Add the flax-water mixture.

3. Sift the cinnamon, nutmeg, and salt into a separate bowl, and then stirinto the wet mixture. Attach the oats and raisins, and fold in.

4. From 3 to 4 tbsp. batter into a ball and press lightly to flatten onto the baking sheet. Repeat, spacing thc cookies 2 to 3 inches apart. Bake for12 minutes until golden brown.

5. Set the cookies in an airtight bag in the fridge.

Nutrition:

Calories: 192 Fat: 16g Carbohydrates: 4g Fiber: 4g Proteins: 4g

Homemade Nutty Fruity Muffins

Preparation time: 15 minutes

Cooking time: 30 minutes

Servings: 6

Ingredients:

- 1 teaspoon coconut oil, for greasing muffin tins (optional)
- 2 tbsp. almond butter, or sunflower seed butter
- ¼ cup non-dairy milk
- 1 orange, peeled
- 1 carrot, coarsely chopped
- 2 tbsp. chopped dried apricots, or other dried fruit
- 3 tablespoons molasses
- 2 tablespoons ground flaxseed
- 1 teaspoon apple cider vinegar
- 1 teaspoon pure vanilla extract
- ½ teaspoon ground cinnamon
- ½ teaspoon ground ginger (optional)
- ¼ teaspoon ground nutmeg (optional)
- ¼ teaspoon allspice (optional)
- ¾ cup rolled oats, or whole-grain flour
- 1 teaspoon baking powder
- ½ teaspoon baking soda Mix-Ins (Optional) :
- ½ cup rolled oats
- 2 tbsp. raisins, or other chopped dried fruit
- 2 tablespoons sunflower seeds

Directions:

1. Preheat the oven to 350F. Prepare a 6-cup muffin tin by rubbing the insides of the cups with coconut oil or using silicone or paper muffincups.

2. Purée the nut butter, milk, orange, carrot, apricots, molasses, flaxseed, vinegar, vanilla, cinnamon, ginger, nutmeg, and allspice in a foodprocessor until somewhat smooth.

3. Grind the oats in a clean coffee grinder until they're the consistency of flour (or use whole-grain flour). In a bowl, mix the oats with the bakingpowder and baking soda.

4. Mix the wet ingredients into the dry ingredients until just combined.Fold in the mix-ins (if using).

5. Set about ¼ cup batter into each muffin cup and bake for 30 minutes.

Nutrition:

Calories: 287 Fat: 23g Carbohydrates: 11g Fiber: 6g Proteins: 8g

Vanilla Flavored Whole Grain Muffins

Preparation time: 15 minutes

Cooking time: 20 minutes

Servings: 12

Ingredients:

- 1 teaspoon coconut oil, for greasing muffin tins (optional)
- 2 tablespoons nut butter or seed butter
- 1½ cups unsweetened applesauce
- ⅓ cup coconut sugar
- ½ cup non-dairy milk
- 2 tablespoons ground flaxseed
- 1 teaspoon apple cider vinegar
- 1 teaspoon pure vanilla extract
- 2 cups whole-grain flour
- 1 teaspoon baking soda
- ½ teaspoon baking powder
- 1 teaspoon ground cinnamon
- Pinch sea salt
- ½ cup walnuts, chopped

Toppings (Optional):
- ¼ cup walnuts
- ¼ cup coconut sugar
- ½ teaspoon ground cinnamon

Directions:

1. Preheat the oven to 350F. Prepare two 6-cup muffin tins by rubbing the insides of the cups with coconut oil or using silicone or paper muffin cups.

2. In a large bowl, mix the nut butter, applesauce, coconut sugar, milk, flaxseed, vinegar, and vanilla until thoroughly combined, or purée in a food processor or blender.

3. In a bowl, sift together the flour, baking soda, baking powder,

4.   cinnamon, salt, and chopped walnuts.

5.   Merge the dry ingredients into the wet ingredients until just combined.

6.   Set about ¼ cup batter into each muffin cup and sprinkle with thetopping of your choice (if using).

7.   Bake for 15 to 20 minutes. The applesauce creates a very moist base, sothe muffins may take longer, depending on how heavy your muffin tinsare.

Nutrition:

Calories: 287 Fat: 12g Carbohydrates: 8g Fiber: 6g Proteins: 8g

Coconut Banana Sandwich with Raspberry Spread

Preparation time: 10 minutes

Cooking time: 30 minutes

Servings: 8

Ingredients:

French toast:
- 1 banana & 1 cup coconut milk
- 1 teaspoon pure vanilla extract
- ¼ teaspoon ground nutmeg & ½ teaspoon ground cinnamon
- 1½ Teaspoons arrowroot powder or flour
- Pinch sea salt & 8 slices whole-grain bread

Raspberry Syrup:
- 1 cup fresh or frozen raspberries
- 2 tablespoons water or pure fruit juice
- 1 to 2 tablespoons maple syrup or coconut sugar (optional)

Directions:

1. Preheat the oven to 350F.

2. In a shallow bowl, purée or mash the banana well. Mix in the coconutmilk, vanilla, nutmeg, cinnamon, arrowroot, and salt.

3. Dip the slices of bread in the banana mixture, and then lay them out ina 13-by-9-inch baking dish.

4. Pour any leftover banana mixture over the bread and put the dish in theoven. Bake for about 30 minutes.

5. Serve topped with raspberry syrup.

6. Heat the raspberries in a small pot with the water and the maple syrup(if using) on medium heat.

7. Leave to simmer, stirring occasionally and breaking up the berries, for 15 to 20 minutes, until the liquid has reduced.

Nutrition:

Calories: 166 Fat: 15g Carbohydrates: 7g Fiber: 4g Proteins: 5g

APPLE TOASTED SWEET SANDWICH

Preparation time: 5 minutes

Cooking time: 20 minutes

Servings: 2

Ingredients:

- 1 to 2 teaspoons coconut oil
- ½ teaspoon ground cinnamon
- 1 tablespoon maple syrup or coconut sugar
- 1 apple, cored and thinly sliced
- 2 slices whole-grain bread

Directions:

1. In a large bowl, merge the coconut oil, cinnamon, and maple syruptogether.

2. Add the apple slices and toss with your hands to coat them.

3. To pan fry the toast, place the apple slices in a medium skillet onmedium-high and cook for about 5 minutes.

4. Cook the bread in the same skillet for 2 to 3 minutes on each side. Topthe toast with the apples. Alternatively, you can bake the toast.

5. Use your hands to rub each slice of bread with some of the coconut oilmixture on both sides.

6. Lay them on a small baking sheet, top with the coated apples, and put in the oven or toaster oven at 350F (180C) for 15 to 20 minutes, or untilthe apples have softened.

Nutrition:

Calories: 187 Fat: 18g Carbohydrates: 7g Fiber: 4g Proteins: 4g

Dried Cranberry Almond Bowl

Preparation time: 10 minutes

Cooking time: 0 minutes

Servings: 5

Ingredients:

Muesli:

- 1 cup rolled oats
- 1 cup spelt flakes, or quinoa flakes, or more rolled oats
- 2 cups puffed cereal
- ¼ cup sunflower seeds
- ¼ cup almonds
- ¼ cup raisins
- ¼ cup dried cranberries
- ¼ cup chopped dried figs
- ¼ cup unsweetened shredded coconut
- ¼ cup non-dairy chocolate chips
- 1 to 3 Teaspoons ground cinnamon

Bowl:

- ½ cup non-dairy milk, or unsweetened applesauce
- ¾ cup muesli
- ½ cup berries

Directions:

1. Put the muesli ingredients in a container or bag and shake.

2. Combine the muesli and bowl ingredients in a bowl or to-go container.

Nutrition:

Calories: 441 Fat: 20g Carbohydrates: 13g Fiber: 13g Proteins: 10g

CHOCOLATE BANANA BREAKFAST BOWL

Preparation time: 5 minutes

Cooking time: 25 minutes

Servings: 4

Ingredients:

- 1 cup quinoa
- 1 tsp. ground cinnamon
- 1 cup non-dairy milk
- 1 cup water
- 1 large banana
- 2 to 3 tbsp. unsweetened cocoa powder
- 1 to 2 tbsp. almond butter, or other vegan butter
- 1 tbsp. ground flaxseed, or chia or hemp seeds
- 2 tablespoons walnuts
- ¼ cup raspberries

Directions:

1. Bring the quinoa, cinnamon, milk, and water in a medium pot. Set to aboil over high heat, and then turn down low and simmer, secured, for 25 to 30 minutes.

2. Purée or press the banana in a bowl and stir in the cocoa powder,almond butter, and flaxseed.

3. To serve, set 1 cup cooked quinoa into a bowl, set with half thepudding and half the walnuts and raspberries.

Nutrition:

Calories: 392 Fat: 19g Carbohydrates: 9g Fiber: 10g Proteins: 12g

FRESH MINT AND COCONUT FRUIT SALAD

Preparation time: 5 minutes

Cooking time: 5 minutes

Servings: 1

Ingredients:

- 1 orange, zested and juiced
- ¼ cup whole-wheat couscous, or corn couscous
- 1 cup assorted berries (strawberries, blackberries, blueberries)
- ½ cup cubed melon (cantaloupe or honeydew)
- 1 tablespoon maple syrup or coconut sugar (optional)
- 1 tablespoon fresh mint, minced (optional)
- 1 tablespoon unsweetened coconut flakes

Directions:

1. Put the orange juice in a small pot, add half the zest, and bring to a boil.

2. Put the dry couscous in a small bowl and pour the boiling orange juice over it. If there isn't enough juice to fully submerge the couscous, addjust enough boiling water to do so.

3. Cover the bowl with a plate or seal with wrap and let steep for 5minutes.

4. In a medium bowl, set the berries and melon with the maple syrup (if using) and the rest of the zest. You can either keep the fruit cool or heatit lightly in the small pot you used for the orange juice.

5. When the couscous is soft, remove the cover and fluff it with a fork.Top with the fruit, fresh mint, and coconut.

Nutrition:

Calories: 496 Fat: 22g Carbohydrates: 7g Fiber: 14g Proteins: 11g

Nutty Fruity Breakfast Bowl

Preparation time: 15 minutes

Cooking time: 30 minutes

Servings: 5

Ingredients:

- 2 cups rolled oats
- ¾ cup whole-grain flour
- 1 tablespoon ground cinnamon
- 1 teaspoon ground ginger (optional)
- ½ cup sunflower seeds, or walnuts, chopped
- ½ cup almonds, chopped
- ½ cup pumpkin seeds & ½ cup unsweetened shredded coconut
- 1¼ cups pure fruit juice (cranberry, apple, or something similar)
- ½ cup raisins, or dried cranberries
- ½ cup goji berries (optional)

Directions:

1. Preheat the oven to 350F.

2. Mix the oats, flour, cinnamon, ginger, sunflower seeds, almonds,pumpkin seeds, and coconut in a large bowl.

3. Dust the juice over the mixture and stir until it's just moistened. You might need a bit more or a bit less liquid, depending on how much youroats and flour absorb.

4. Scatter the granola on a large baking sheet (the more spread out it is thebetter) and put it in the oven. Use a spatula to turn the granola so that the middle gets dried out. Let the granola bake for 30 minutes.

5. Set the granola out of the oven and stir in the raisins and goji berries (ifusing).

6. Set leftovers in an airtight container for up to 2 weeks.

Nutrition:

Calories: 398 Fat: 25g Carbohydrates: 9g Fiber: 8gProteins: 10g

Peppery Mushroom Tomato Bowl

Preparation time: 10 minutes

Cooking time: 15 minutes

Servings: 1

Ingredients:

- 1 tsp. olive oil, or 1 tbsp. vegetable broth or water
- ½ cup sliced mushrooms
- Pinch sea salt & ½ cup chopped zucchini
- ½ cup chickpeas (cooked or canned)
- 1 teaspoon smoked paprika, or regular paprika
- 1 teaspoon turmeric
- 1 tablespoon nutritional yeast (optional)
- Freshly ground black pepper
- ½ cup cherry tomatoes, chopped
- ¼ cup fresh parsley, sliced

Directions:

1. Heat a large skillet to medium-high. Once the skillet is hot, attach theolive oil and mushrooms, along with the sea salt to help them soften, and sauté, stirring occasionally, 7 to 8 minutes.

2. Attach the zucchini to the skillet.

3. If you're using canned chickpeas, wash and drain them. Press the chickpeas with a potato masher, fork, or your fingers. Add them to the skillet and cook until they are heated through.

4. Set the paprika, turmeric, and nutritional yeast over the chickpeas, andstir to combinc.

5. Set in the black pepper, cherry tomatoes and fresh parsley at the end.

Nutrition:

Calories: 265 Fat: 18g Carbohydrates: 7g Fiber: 12g Proteins: 16g

Roasted Beets and Carrot with Avocado Dip

Preparation time: 10 minutes

Cooking time: 30 minutes

Servings: 2

Ingredients:

Avocado Dip:

- 1 avocado
- 1 tablespoon apple cider vinegar
- ¼ to ½ cup water
- 2 tablespoons nutritional yeast
- 1 tsp. dried dill, or 1 tablespoon fresh dill
- Pinch sea salt
- Roasted Veg:
- 1 small sweet potato, peeled and cubed
- 2 small beets, peeled and cubed
- 2 small carrots, peeled and cubed
- 1 teaspoon sea salt
- 1 teaspoon dried oregano
- ¼ teaspoon cayenne pepper
- Pinch freshly ground black pepper

Directions:

1. In a blender, purée the avocado with the other dip ingredients, usingjust enough water to get a smooth, creamy texture.

2. Alternately, you can mash the avocado thoroughly in a large bowl, thenstir in the rest of the dip ingredients.

3. Preheat the oven to 350F.

4. Put the sweet potato, beets, and carrots in a large pot with a small amount of water and set to a boil. Boil for 15 minutes, until they're justbarely soft, and then drain.

5.   Sprinkle the salt, oregano, cayenne, and pepper over them and stirgently to combine.

6.   Set the vegetables on a large baking sheet and roast them in the oven for 10 to 15 minutes, until they've browned around the edges.

7.   Serve the veg with the avocado dip on the side.

Nutrition:

Calories: 335 Fat: 32g Carbohydrates: 11g Proteins: 11g Fiber: 16g

RAISIN OAT COOKIES

Preparation time: 10 minutes

Cooking time: 9 minutes

Servings: 2

Ingredients:

- ⅓ cup almond butter & ½ cup maple sugar
- ¼ cup unsweetened applesauce
- 1 teaspoon vanilla extract & ⅓ cup sorghum flour
- ⅔ cups oat flour & ½ teaspoon baking soda
- ½ cup raisins & 1 cup rolled oats
- ½ teaspoon ground cinnamon
- ¼ teaspoon salt (optional)

Directions:

1. Preheat the oven to 350F (180C). Line two baking sheets with parchment paper. Whisk together the almond butter, maple sugar, and applesauce in alarge bowl until smooth.

2. Mix in the remaining ingredients and keep whisking until a stiff doughforms.

3. Divide and roll the dough into 24 small balls, then arrange the balls inthe baking sheets. Keep a little space between each two balls. Bash them with your hands to make them form like cookies.

4. Bake in the warm oven for 9 minutes or until crispy. Flip the cookieshalfway through the

5. Cooking time.

6. Detach them from the oven and allow cooling for 10 minutes beforeserving.

Nutrition:

Calories: 140 Fat: 56.0g Carbohydrates: 224.1g Proteins: 45.5g Fiber: 30.5g

Oat Scones

Preparation time: 15 minutes

Cooking time: 22 minutes

Servings: 12

Ingredients:

- 1 teaspoon apple cider vinegar
- ½ cup unsweetened soy milk
- 1 teaspoon vanilla extract
- 3 cups oat flour
- 2 tablespoons baking powder
- ½ cup maple sugar
- ½ teaspoon salt (optional)
- ⅓ cup almond butter
- ½ cup unsweetened applesauce

Directions:

1. Preheat the oven to 350F (180C). Line a baking sheet with parchmentpaper.

2. Combine cider vinegar and soy milk in a bowl. Stir to mix well. Letstand for a few minutes to curdle, and then mix in the vanilla.

3. Merge the flour, baking powder, sugar, and salt (if desired) in a secondbowl. Stir to mix well.

4. Combine the almond butter and applesauce in a third bowl. Stir to mixwell.

5. Gently fold the applesauce mixture in the flour mixture, and then stir inthe milk mixture.

6. Scoop the mixture on the baking sheet with an ice-cream scoop to make12 scones. Drizzle them with a touch of water.

7. Bake in the warm oven for 22 minutes or until puffed and lightlybrowned. Flip the scones halfway through the

8.   Cooking time.

9.   Remove them from the oven and allow cooling for 10 minutes beforeserving.

Nutrition:

Calories: 177 Fat: 6.0g Carbohydrates: 26.6g Proteins: 5.4g Fiber: 2.5g

GOLDEN MILK

Preparation time: 5 minutes

Cooking time: 0 minutes

Servings: 2

Ingredients:

- ½ teaspoon ground cinnamon
- ½ teaspoon ground turmeric
- ½ teaspoon grated fresh ginger
- 1 teaspoon maple syrup
- 1 cup unsweetened coconut milk
- Ground black pepper, to taste
- 2 tablespoons water

Directions:

1. Combine all the ingredients in a saucepan. Stir to mix well.

2. Heat over medium heat for 5 minutes. Keep stirring during the heating.

3. Allow to cool then pour the mixture in a blender. Pulse until creamyand smooth. Serve immediately.

Nutrition:

Calories: 577 Fat: 57.3g Carbohydrates: 19.7g Proteins: 5.7g Fiber: 6.1g

Mango Agua Fresca

Preparation time: 5 minutes

Cooking time: 0 minutes

Servings: 2

Ingredients:

- 2 fresh mangoes, diced
- 1½ cups water
- 1 teaspoon fresh lime juice
- Maple syrup, to taste
- 2 cups ice
- 2 slices fresh lime, for garnish
- 2 fresh mint sprigs, for garnish

Directions:

1. Put the mangoes, lime juice, maple syrup, and water in a blender.Process until creamy and smooth.

2. Divide the beverage into two glasses, and then garnish each glass withice, lime slice, and mint sprig before serving.

Nutrition:

Calories: 230 Fat: 1.3g Carbohydrates: 57.7g Proteins: 2.8g Fiber: 5.4g

CLASSIC SWITCHEL

Preparation time: 5 minutes

Cooking time: 0 minutes

Servings: 5

Ingredients:

- 1-inch piece ginger, minced
- 2 tablespoons apple cider vinegar
- 2 tablespoons maple syrup
- 4 cups water
- ¼ teaspoon sea salt (optional)

Directions:

1. Combine all the ingredients in a glass. Stir to mix well.

2. Serve immediately.

Nutrition:

Calories: 110 Fat: 0g Carbohydrates: 28.0g Proteins: 0g Fiber: 0g

Easy and Fresh Mango Madness

Preparation time: 5 minutes

Cooking time: 0 minutes

Servings: 5

Ingredients:

- 1 cup chopped mango
- 1 cup chopped peach
- 1 banana
- 1 cup strawberries
- 1 carrot, peeled and chopped
- 1 cup water

Directions:

1. Arrange all the ingredients in a food processor, then blitz until glossyand smooth.

2. Serve immediately.

Nutrition:

Calories: 376 Fat: 22.0g Carbohydrates: 19.0g Fiber: 14.0g Proteins: 5.0g

Blueberry Coconut Milkshake

Preparation time: 5 minutes

Cooking time: 0 minutes

Servings: 2

Ingredients:

- 1 can coconut milk
- 1½ cups frozen blueberries
- 1 tbsp. maple syrup
- 1 tsp. vanilla extract

Directions:

1. Use a blender to mix all the ingredients until smooth. If it's too thick,add a little water. Serve immediately.

Nutrition:

Calories: 496 Fat: 22g Carbohydrates: 7g Fiber: 14g Proteins: 11g

Conclusion

Eating more vegan foods, by definition, will lead you to eat less saturated fatand overall calories than you would on a non-vegan diet. If you're a vegetarian or vegan or are just curious about the possibilities of plant-based nutrition, we hope that we've shown you that just because something is plant-based doesn't mean it is boring. There are so many great vegan dishes out there! Rather than being overwhelmed by everything on the market. Try to focus on the core principles of cooking with whole foods and substituting foranimal products where possible. You might be amazed at how fast you gain confidence in making your recipes. Vegan food that is good for you is delicious food!

For the average adult, a diet of non-animal-based proteins and essential fats issufficient to meet all nutritional needs.

Vegan and vegetarian diets are rich in essential fatty acids, vitamins, iron andcalcium, consumed here in higher concentrations than non-vegetarian diets.

Vegan foods provide all the nutrients necessary for human health. Veganfoods are entirely cholesterol-free. Vegan plant-based proteins have beenshown to lower blood sugars in people with diabetes, reduce serum cholesterol levels and even alleviate arthritis symptoms.

It's radiant to get tied up in the diet trends, but if we follow the basic principles of healthy eating, we will always be on course. Consuming overflow of fruits and vegetables, whole grains, nuts, seeds and legumes, unprocessed lean protein such as beans and tofu, plenty of water and low saturated fat will be your ticket to good health. Whatever you choose to call it

– vegan, vegetarian or flexitarian.

The recipes in this book are fun, delicious and inspiring! Cooking vegan foodis easy. The hardest part is being consistent. You'll want to choose your ingredients wisely and be prepared to cook often. I hope that my tips encourage you to continue your plant-based journey.